TROPICAL RAINFORESTS

D1523593

TROPICAL RAINFORESTS
ENDANGERED ENVIRONMENT

James D. Nations

Franklin Watts 1988
New York / London / Toronto / Sydney

Maps and drawings by John V. Cotter

Photographs courtesy of: James D. Nations, except
the following: Linda Sims: p. 15; Donald R. Perry:
p. 24; Chip Clark: p. 30; Merlin D. Tuttle, Bat
Conservation International: p. 32; Photo Researchers:
p. 37 (Tom McHugh); Henry Rasof: pp. 45, 49, 74;
Chris B. Rollins: p. 52; Melvin Calvin: p. 57;
AP/Wide World Photos: p. 83; UPI/Bettmann Newsphotos:
p. 96; Mac Chapin/Cultural Survival: p. 115.

The publisher wishes to thank Dr. Merlin D. Tuttle,
science director of Bat Conservation International,
for his assistance in preparing the section on bats.

Library of Congress Cataloging-in-Publication Data

Nations, James D.
Tropical rainforests / James D. Nations ; [maps and drawings by
John V. Cotter].
p.   cm.
Bibliography: p.
Includes index.
Summary: Describes the oldest and most complex of ecosystems, the
tropical rainforest—its wonders, its importance, its people, and
the threats against which we must protect it.
ISBN 0-531-10604-7
1. Rain forest ecology—Juvenile literature.   2. Rain forests—
Juvenile literature.   [1. Rain forest ecology.   2. Rain forests.]
I. Cotter, John V., ill.   II. Title.
QH541.5.R27N37   1988
574.5'2642—dc19   88-5695   CIP   AC

CHB

Contents

For Christopher and Jamie,
visitors to the tropical rainforest,

and for Michu, Chan K'in,
Enrique, and Chan Nuk,
who live there.

*We have not inherited
the Earth from our parents,
we have borrowed it
from our children.*

World Conservation Strategy
International Union for
the Conservation of Nature
and Natural Resources

Int20buction

THE YEAR A.D. 2090

Speeding toward home from a long expedition in space, the astronauts congratulate one another as the blue Earth spins into view. After years within the metal skin of their spacecraft, they celebrate the sight of the natural world where they were born.

As their ship nears Earth, the astronauts watch giant swirls of clouds build into storms over the Pacific Ocean. The navigator points out the continent of Africa and the beige sands of the Sahara Desert. But the crew's eyes fix on an uneven band of green that encircles the globe at the equator.

"What you are looking at," the expedition's biologist tells them, "is the oldest and most complex collection of life on our planet—the tropical rainforest."

"Only a century ago," he says, "tropical rainforests formed a belt of vegetation that went around the earth, wherever the land was low and the climate warm and wet. But today, as you can see, the belt is broken. Large areas

of tropical rainforest were destroyed during the twentieth century."

The navigator interrupts. "But if tropical rainforests are so ancient and complex," he asks, "why did people destroy them during the twentieth century?"

"It's a long story," says the biologist, "but take it from me, we're lucky that rainforests still exist. They protect the biological blueprint for some of our most important food crops, and they're the home of half of all the kinds of plants and animals on earth. They also play an important role in regulating the global climate. In fact, tropical rainforests may be the most important environment on earth. People didn't always know that."

AN ENDANGERED ENVIRONMENT

Although tropical rainforests cover less than 8 percent of our planet's surface, more different kinds of animals and plants live there than any other place on earth.[1] These forests are vital sources of food, fuel, shelter, medicines, and other useful products. As the expedition's biologist points out, tropical rainforests provide a wealth of benefits to human beings, and they are one of our most valuable natural resources.

Yet the world's tropical rainforests are being destroyed. Around the world—in Africa, Asia, and Latin America—rainforests are being cut down and burned at the rate of at least 25,000 square miles (65,000 square kilometers) per year. Combined into one block, this would represent a forest the size of West Virginia wiped out every year.

Tropical rainforest destruction results from complex combinations of social, economic, and biological causes. Rainforests are threatened by expanding farmlands, growing populations, and the harvesting of natural products such as timber, palms, minerals, and wildlife.[2] As these forests are destroyed, the earth loses the plants and animals that live in them, and human beings lose the benefits that the forests can bring. Eradicating these forests also means destroying the communities and traditions of tribal people whose ancestors have lived in rainforests for thousands of years.

Fortunately, we are beginning to realize the important role that tropical rainforests play in improving our lives and in maintaining the health of our planet. Whether or not these unique environments survive to benefit future generations of life on earth depends on how we treat them during the next few decades. Conserving these forests, their wildlife, and the people who live within them is one of the most important challenges we face in the twentieth century.[3]

1
What Are
Tropical
Rainforests?

Our planet is home to hundreds of kinds of plants and animals interacting with the physical world that surrounds them. Scientists call these interactions "ecological systems," or *ecosystems*. They speak of desert ecosystems, arctic ecosystems, and the ecosystems of forests, oceans, and meadows.

Of all the ecosystems on land, the most unchanging and most complex is the *tropical rainforest*. Rainforests are dense green webs of plants and animals that occur along the earth's equator. People sometimes call these forests jungles.

Asking scientists to describe rainforests would net you a variety of answers depending on the scientists' disciplines. A botanist would tell you that tropical rainforests grow in warm, wet regions of Central and South America, Africa, and Southeast Asia. He or she might say that tropical rainforests grow on well-drained soils, mostly at low altitudes, but on some mountainsides up to 4,500 feet (1,400 meters). They would probably tell you that rain falls every month of the year in tropical rainforests.

A zoologist might tell you that tropical rainforests are home to more than half of all the animals on earth, that a patch of tropical rainforest may have ten times more different kinds (species) of animals and plants than a patch of forest in New York or Montana.

An adventurer returning from a visit to a tropical rainforest might tell you that they are steamy, dark, and mysterious, filled with millions of fascinating plants, monkeys, snakes, and insects.

An anthropologist would probably say that tropical rainforests are home to some of the oldest and most interesting societies on earth—pygmies in Africa, Indian hunters in South America, isolated tribesmen in Borneo.

All these people and all their answers would be correct. But even taken together, these answers fail to capture the complexity of the tropical rainforest, because rainforests are the most diverse ecosystem on earth. For more than 60 million years, they have preserved ancient forms of life and served as a continual source of new species of plants and animals. Tropical rainforests are the greatest single reservoir of plants and animals on our planet. They are the natural habitat of hundreds of thousands of undiscovered forms of life.

An area of tropical rainforest 2.5 acres (1 hectare) in size may support two hundred different kinds of trees, as well as hundreds of kinds of ferns, vines, shrubs, and fungi. The same plot of tropical forest will serve as the home of thousands of species of animals. Monkeys, exotic birds, butterflies, beetles, frogs, bats, and spotted cats have inhabited tropical rainforests longer than human beings have lived on earth.

Because they contain so many different species of plants and animals, tropical rainforests are the most important ecosystem for the evolution of life on earth. If even a small percentage of these millions of kinds of animals and plants are eradicated, the course of biological evolution will be changed forever.

HOW MANY MILLIONS OF SPECIES?

The number of species found in tropical rainforests exceeds the number found in all other land ecosystems *combined*. But just how many species of plants and animals live in the world's tropical rainforests is still a matter of debate. We know that tropical rainforests are home to half of all the plant and animal species on earth, but we don't know how many species that means.

Biologists have traditionally estimated the total number of species of plants and animals in the world's tropical rainforests to be between 5 million and 10 million. But a recent study of the rainforest of Panama and Peru by Dr. Terry Erwin of the Smithsonian Institution indicates that the actual number is far higher than this. Erwin devised a system for collecting the insects from the treetops of tropical rainforests using pesticides. He raises a canister filled with insecticide up into the trees and releases the chemicals as a fog. Although the insecticide does not harm larger animals, it kills thousands of insects as it spreads through the vegetation. The insects fall out of the trees like rain onto sheets placed on the forest floor by Erwin and his assistants.

Through careful examination of thousands of insect specimens brought down from the trees in this fashion, Erwin estimates that rainforests may contain as many as 30 million species of insects alone, rather than the 1.5 million scientists had always guessed. And we are talking here only of the *insects* of the forest! The majority of all reptile and amphibian species and of all trees also live in tropical rainforests.[1]

By any calculation, only a small percentage of the plants and animals that live in the earth's tropical rainforests have ever been scientifically examined. This means that tropical rainforests hide millions of unknown species— more than scientists have described and named since Linnaeus began the process of applying scientific names 230 years ago.

In this setup designed by Dr. Terry Erwin, insects killed by the insecticide spray fall into the net.

There is no question that many new sources of food, medicines, fuel, and industrial products remain undiscovered in the world's tropical rainforests. Some of these unknown species could be vitally important to our future. Tropical rainforests have already provided us with some of our most important food crops and medicines, a topic we'll examine in detail in chapter 3.

Scientists have determined some of the causes of the incredible diversity of tropical rainforests. In the first place, rainforests are an ancient ecosystem. As Catherine Caufield writes in her book *In the Rainforest*, "Evolution has rolled on in many rainforests for the past 60 million years, making them the oldest communities on earth."[2] Rainforests have existed for millions of years, and this long period of time has allowed new species to evolve from previous ones.

Another reason for the rainforest's diversity is its constantly hot and moist climate. Rainforests are gigantic hothouses. When nature allows *photosynthesis* to remain high year round, everything grows all the time. (Photosynthesis is the conversion of the sun's energy to carbohydrates, the plants' food, by green plants). The enormous quantities of sunlight, warmth, and rain in the earth's tropical rainforests are what make them so wealthy in plant and animal life. Tropical rainforests appear only where these conditions of climate, temperature, and rainfall coincide.[3]

WHY ARE THERE TROPICAL RAINFORESTS?

By the broadest definition, a tropical forest is any forest that grows between the Tropic of Cancer and the Tropic of Capricorn, two imaginary lines that circle the globe near the equator and define the area where the earth is closest to the sun.

Within this *tropical zone* (which we usually call the tropics), the sun's rays beat down on the earth from almost directly overhead. By contrast, in areas north or south of the tropics, the sun's rays must pass through a thicker layer of atmosphere, and sunlight is less intense. We call these other regions of the earth the temperate zones.

In the tropics, the high angle of the sun generates more warmth and solar energy than in the temperate zones. The average difference between the hottest and coldest months of the year is much less than the difference in temperature between night and day. For this reason, biologist Marston Bates called the tropics the region of the earth "where winter never comes."[4]

The tropics are covered by a variety of types of forests. These are not accidents of nature but depend upon factors of altitude and moisture. Short scrub forests covered with thorns may grow in tropical regions with low rainfall. Where the land and ocean come together and the shoreline is periodically flooded with a mixture of seawater and fresh water from rivers, we may find the tangled forest of trees and shrubs that scientists call mangroves. On tall, cool mountain tops with plenty of rainfall, we may find tropical pine forests not unlike the pine forests of the United States or Europe.

Tropical mountains and slopes shrouded in clouds and mist much of the day may be covered in cloud forest. And in tropical regions where rain falls only during certain months of the year, trees may temporarily lose their leaves. We call these seasonal forests, or tropical deciduous forests.

What exactly do we mean, then, by tropical rainforest? In some low regions of the tropics, the amount of rain in a year reaches at least 80 inches (2 meters) and may exceed *four* times that much. Where this yearly rainfall is distributed throughout all months of the year, and at least 8 inches (20 centimeters) of rain falls in every month, the forest is luxurious and complex. The trees may reach a height of 150 feet (46 meters), as tall as a fifteen-story building.

Still, almost all tropical rainforests receive less rainfall in some months of the year than they do in others. These wet and dry seasons cause the vegetation to go through different periods of flowering and fruiting, although the

Above: *in this tropical pine forest in Honduras, one type of tree—the pine—is dominant. The same amount of space in a tropical rainforest would contain an enormous diversity of species of trees.*
Right: *tropical rainforest in Brazil.*

temperature within the forest remains steady. Humidity is high and even throughout the year. The combined effects of this high temperature and high humidity produce the abundance of plant and animal life that makes tropical rainforests so important to life on earth. This diversity is the most striking feature of tropical rainforests.

TWO MAJOR TYPES OF RAINFOREST

Not all tropical rainforests are alike. Although they appear where certain conditions of temperature and rainfall coincide, some of these forests receive more rain than others. The wettest of them—160 inches (4 meters) or more of rainfall per year—have hardly any dry season and are called equatorial evergreen forests. They appear along the earth's equator in South America, West Africa, and Asia.

Rainforests that get less rainfall (but at least 40 inches—1 meter—per year) are located farther from the earth's equator and are sometimes called tropical moist forests or semideciduous tropical forests. In this book, we will call both types of these forests tropical rainforests.

Defining the boundaries of the rainforest is a difficult task. At their edges, tropical rainforests blend into other types of tropical forest. At the coast, they may grade into

A combination of intense sunlight, high temperatures, and heavy rainfall along the earth's tropical belt produces the dense vegetation formations called tropical rainforests. Although they cover less than 8 percent of the planet's surface, tropical rainforests are home to more than half of all types of plants and animals on earth.

(20)

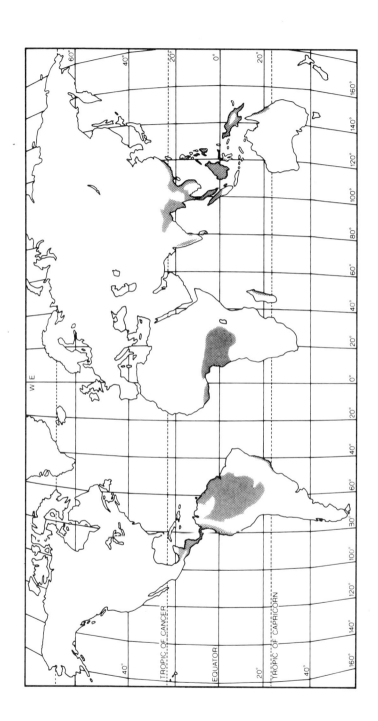

mangrove forest. With increasing altitude, they may gradually blend into pine forests or cloud forests. In regions of less rainfall, they blend into deciduous, or seasonal, tropical forest. Usually, these other types of tropical forest are home to fewer plant and animal species than the wetter tropical rainforest.

WHERE ARE TROPICAL RAINFORESTS?

The belt of rainforest around the Earth's tropical zone is not continuous. It is interrupted by the oceans, by chains of tall mountains, and by areas of low rainfall. In fact, most of our planet's tropical rainforest occurs in three main blocks.

The largest of these blocks lies in Latin America, the site of more than half the world's tropical rainforest. Brazil has the largest share, but rainforest also appears in Ecuador, Bolivia, Peru, Colombia, Venezuela, the Guyanas, and in the republics of Central America. In all, tropical rainforest covers more than 1.5 million square miles (3.9 million square kilometers) of Central and South America.

Southeast Asia has the second largest block of tropical rainforest, with about one-fifth of the earth's total (500,000 square miles, or 1.3 million square kilometers). Most of Asia's rainforest appears in the countries of Indonesia, Malaysia, Papua New Guinea, and the Philippines.

And, finally, more than 380,000 square miles (950,000 square kilometers) of tropical rainforest, roughly one-seventh of the world's total, occurs in Africa, chiefly in West Africa and Madagascar.[5]

Just how much of this tropical rainforest will still exist a century from now will be determined by the actions of human beings now alive and those who will be born during the next ten to twenty years. As we'll see in the following chapters, the survival or destruction of this ancient ecosystem will have serious impacts on our lives as human beings and on the future of life on our planet.

2
Wonders of the Tropical Rainforest

In these forests lies a virtually limitless supply of excitement, joy, and wonder.

Thomas E. Lovejoy, World Wildlife Fund

CLIMBING INTO THE CANOPY

On both sides of the trail, giant trees stand dripping with rain. Thick vines twist down from a forest canopy that extends as far as you can see into a green wall of vegetation. Overhead, a blue and green parrot feeds on jungle fruit, tossing aside pieces that fall 100 feet (30 meters) to the forest floor below. Insects whine and hum and buzz with a hundred different voices, and a tiny brocket deer flashes across the trail into the undergrowth, disappearing into shadow. The air smells like a mixture of rot and genesis.

Almost unseen in this exotic setting, a man slowly makes his way up a rope draped over a branch of the tallest tree. From the forest floor, he looks like a spider suspended in a web ten stories above the ground. The man is biologist

Donald Perry. The tree he is climbing is in the tropical rainforest of the Osa Peninsula in the Central American country of Costa Rica. But what is he doing and why has he come so far to climb trees?

Dr. Perry has perfected a technique for climbing rainforest trees using ropes, pulleys, and ascenders—special mountain climbers' equipment normally used to scale tall cliffs and steep slopes. The ascenders allow Perry to pull himself slowly up the ropes into the tallest branches of rainforest trees, but they lock in place to prevent him from slipping back down. Once he is ready to climb down, Perry releases the ascenders' grip, and rappels down the rope to the ground. Before Perry created this system, scientists had no reliable way to enter into the world of the forest *canopy*, the highest layer of the tropical rainforest.

Perry carries out scientific research on the rainforest canopy because we know almost nothing about this unexplored region of the rainforest. Now, Perry and other researchers are discovering that *two-thirds* of the plants and animals of the rainforest are seldom found near the ground. Instead, they live in the canopy, far out of reach of earthbound humans. Perry says that as much as 80 percent of the food consumed by rainforest creatures grows within the canopy. The canopy, he continues, is the rainforest's "main level." If the bulk of plants and animals live there, it seems logical that scientists who study them would follow.[1]

LAYERS OF THE TROPICAL FOREST

Tropical rainforests may look like a mass of trees, ferns, and vines extending from the top of the tallest trees to the

*Dr. Donald Perry explores
the rainforest canopy.*

moist forest soil below. But tropical biologists point out that the vegetation of the rainforest can be divided into layers. These layers are not easy to distinguish in real life, but they help researchers analyze the tropical rainforest's complexity.

The layers of the rainforest also help explain its lush diversity, for the variety of layers provide thousands of different natural environments (*habitats*) for the forest's plants and animals.

Biologists usually think of tropical rainforests as having three layers. At the top, where Dr. Perry is headed with his ropes and pulleys, is the canopy. Between the canopy and the ground is the *understory*, filled with small trees, palms, and shrubs. At the bottom is the *forest floor*. The forest floor consists of a layer of debris and rotting vegetation and the thin tropical soil that supports the entire structure of the forest.

With that outline in mind, we can look at each of these layers in turn.

LIFE IN THE CANOPY

Like a huge umbrella, or a living roof spread over a moist, dark forest floor, the canopy of the tropical rainforest serves as a barrier for rainfall and sunlight. It interrupts both rain and sun but allows them to filter through, diffused by its web of giant trees and vines.

As the tallest realm of the tropical rainforest, the canopy forms a continuous green carpet of tree crowns 75 to 150 feet (23 to 45 meters) above the ground. Flying above the rainforest in an airplane, you might imagine the canopy as an undulating ocean of green hiding everything beneath it. Looking up from the forest floor, you might see the canopy as a high, green ceiling that cuts off all but thin streams of sunlight.

In some rainforests, giant trees called *emergents* poke their crowns above the layer of the canopy to spread their

Scientists divide the vegetation of the tropical rainforest into layers, although the layers blend into one another in real life. The tallest layer, the canopy, forms a green ceiling of tree crowns basking in the sunlight. Below the canopy is the understory, a mixed growth of young trees, vines, and palms. The forest floor is covered by plants growing in the fallen debris and rotting vegetation that lie on the rainforest's fragile soil.

branches in the bright tropical sunlight. The tallest of the rainforest trees, they are fully exposed to the high temperatures and strong winds of the tropics.

If the canopy of the rainforest forms a broad roof over the forest floor, the beams that hold the roof in place are the branches and trunks of the rainforest trees. Most rainforest trees grow on slender, towering trunks that break out into huge limbs supporting a dome-shaped crown. They branch out only when they reach the sunlight of the canopy. At ground level, some trees bear broad fans of roots called *buttresses* which rise up like the supporting walls of a cathedral. Buttresses help balance the weight of the tree on the thin tropical rainforest soil.

Within the branches of the rainforest canopy lives a virtual zoo of wildlife. Here you find all manner of creatures clinging to and hanging from the tree branches.

In Latin America, loud howler monkeys and agile spider monkeys travel through the canopy in groups, sometimes dangling from tree limbs by their tails to feed on ripening fruits. In the rainforests of Southeast Asia, gibbons and orangutans swing playfully from branch to branch. In the Guinea rainforest of Africa, red colobus monkeys and their close cousins, black colobus monkeys, graze on leaves of the upper level of the forest. These canopy-dwelling primates rarely venture to the forest floor, but in the treetops they are unmatched in their skill at traveling from tree to tree in search of food.

Also within the canopy live thousands of species of birds. Toucans with preposterous beaks devour fruits and berries, insects, and tiny birds. In Central and South America, huge harpy eagles with hand-sized talons fly from tree to tree, pausing to search for unsuspecting monkeys, sloths, and opossums.

And everywhere inside the canopy, the air is alive with the flashing wings of butterflies, seeking out the sweet nectars of bright jungle flowers. Insects are the most numerous creatures in the canopy.

WITHIN THE UNDERSTORY

Because the canopy absorbs 98 percent of the sunlight that strikes the rainforest, the plants and animals of the understory live in a twilight world where humidity is high and the air barely moves. The amount of moisture in the air rarely falls below 95 percent day or night. Temperatures don't climb as high as they do in the direct sunlight above the canopy, but they still may reach 90 degrees Fahrenheit (32 degrees centigrade). This combination of high humidity and high temperature makes the understory an uncomfortable place for people from other climates.

Like the rainforest canopy, the understory is well populated with vegetation and wildlife. Some of the trees are immature specimens of canopy trees working their way up toward the sunlight. Others are dwarf palms and shrubs that live their entire lives in the emerald twilight of the understory.

Small trees and spined palms are thickest where the canopy is broken so that sunlight reaches the forest floor. When trees fall, they open up long, narrow gaps in the forest and allow shafts of brilliant light to warm the dark understory. The bright sunlight and high temperatures bring to life seeds that have lain dormant on the forest floor. Gradually, the seedlings grow toward the canopy to heal the rainforest's temporary wound.

As in the canopy, insects are everywhere in the understory—crawling, flying, inching their way across leaves, hiding under flowers, disguising themselves as twigs or other animals.

To protect themselves from their enemies, many understory insects adopt disguises or camouflage. Some katydids have flat bodies and large, green wings that make them look like just another leaf on an understory shrub. But watch the leaf long enough and it moves its legs as it feeds on the very plants it looks like, an almost perfect camouflage against predators.

*This katydid resembles a
leaf—or thinks it does.*

Even more effective is the *mimicry* (protective similarity) carried out by the larvae of the sphingid butterfly of Central America. Undisturbed, the green larvae hides itself on the plants of the rainforest understory. But if an animal threatens to eat it, the larvae swells its thorax and swings its head in a convincing imitation of a black and yellow parrot snake. The sudden appearance of a threatening "snake" is enough to scare away even the hungriest of predators.

BATS AND CATS IN THE FOREST

The rainforest understory is also the home of a wealth of tropical bats. Most are insect feeders, catching meals on the wing as they flit silently through the forest. A single bat may eat three thousand insects in one night. Other bats, called nectar-feeders, have powerful eyes and a strong sense of smell. Their enhanced senses guide the bats to flowers that promise sweet sips of nectar, the bats' primary food. In exchange for the flowers' nectar, the bats perform a service for the plants—they pollinate them. As they reach into the flowers to drink the nectar with their long, paintbrush tongues, the bats become covered with the flowers' pollen, which rubs off onto their heads and necks. Then, when the bats land on other flowers of the same species, the pollen grains rub off again, pollinating the other plants to keep the species alive. Wild bananas, for example, depend on bats to pollinate them.

Still other bats feed on jungle fruits. Their well-developed sense of smell helps them search out ripened fruit. They use their incisor teeth to crush the fruit and their tongues to press the fruit against the roof of their mouth to squeeze out the juice and inner pulp. In eating these fruits, bats help spread the seeds of rainforest plants and regenerate the forest.[2] Bats are also critically important to forest regeneration in cleared areas. In these places seeds

An endangered Marianas fruit bat feeds on pollen of a tree on Guam.

dropped by bats account for up to 95 percent of the first new trees, known as pioneer species. When these have grown sufficiently, birds are attracted, and they drop seeds of less hardy trees beneath the other trees. These trees eventually mature, sheltered by the first pioneers. Finally, primates and other large mammals are attracted, completing the reforestation process.[3]

Also living within the understory of the rainforests of Latin America are vampire bats, which live by drinking blood. Stealthily, they travel through the forest under cover of night to seek out jungle mammals. With tiny, razor-sharp teeth they slice off a thin layer of skin and quietly lap up the flowing blood. Anticoagulants in the bats' saliva keep the blood from clotting. Although vampire bats can be serious pests where humans raise livestock such as cattle, they rarely attack people, and screens and mosquito nets are enough to deter them. Less than 1 percent of the nearly one thousand species of bats in the world are vampire bats.

Within the rainforest understory we also find meat-eating cats such as the jaguar and ocelot in Latin America, and the two-spotted palm civet and golden cat of Africa. Some of the smaller cats prey on birds, lizards, and rodents such as agoutis and pacas. Larger cats like the jaguar catch small deer and tapirs by lurking in trees high in the branches, then dropping silently onto the back of their prey.

THE MOIST FOREST FLOOR

The rainforest's luxurious vegetation grows from soil that is surprisingly infertile. Like a beggar in an elegant suit, the rainforest is wearing almost everything it owns. The dense vegetation of the tropical rainforest disguises the fact that the soil of the forest floor is very poor in *nutrients*, the food materials that plants consume. Ninety percent of the tropical rainforest's nutrients are caught up in the vegetation itself, high above the thin topsoil of the forest floor.

Instead of taking up nutrients from deep in the soil, tropical rainforests live off their own debris. Their shallow root system rapidly recycles nutrients that fall to the forest floor in the form of leaves, twigs, limbs, and dead animals and plants. Much of this debris is decomposed by termites and earthworms, but these creatures are joined in their task by bacteria and fungi.

Push aside the thin layer of litter on the rainforest floor and you'll find a dense root mat that looks like a mass of interwoven white threads. The threads are actually a mixture of tiny roots of forest trees and strands of fungi. The roots and fungi work together to capture and recycle the nutrients released by decaying plant and animal matter. This root system is so efficient that almost all the nutrients released by decaying plants are recycled into living plants. This rapid recycling produces the rainforest's paradox of extravagant vegetation growing from infertile soils.

The rainforest floor is also the home of a host of animals willing to graze along the forest floor or root in the soil for their food. In Africa, giant forest hogs weighing 600 pounds (300 kilograms) travel in herds of twenty, eating the leaves and shoots of low-growing shrubs. In Southeast Asia, black and white tapirs browse the river banks to feed on grasses, buds, soft twigs, and fruits. The tapirs are fine swimmers, and they spend much of their time in jungle rivers, cooling off and eating aquatic plants. In the rainforests of West Africa, lowland gorillas spend most of their lives on the forest floor, although they may climb into the understory to feed and into low trees to sleep at night.

Also on the rainforest floor hide long-fanged, poisonous snakes such as the fer-de-lance and bushmaster of Latin

A variety of mammals live on the rainforest floor, including this tapir (top) from Mexico and this capybara from Trinidad.

America, the latter up to 12 feet (3.7 meters) long. They feed on rats, frogs, lizards, and small mammals like the agouti and are much less common than some movies would have you believe.

Although you would expect to find them only in the canopy and undergrowth, birds also live on the floor of the tropical rainforest. Pheasants, peacocks, and flightless cassowaries search the forest floor for berries, fruits, seeds, and insects. One Southeast Asian rainforest bird, appropriately called the jungle fowl, is the ancestor of our domestic chicken.

Insects are the most numerous of all creatures on the forest floor, as they are on all other layers of the rainforest. They play a crucial role in breaking down the nutrients of rainforest debris and recycling them to living plants. But some insects are unwilling to wait for the forest to produce debris. Leaf-cutter ants climb tree trunks in single file and scissor out pieces of leaves with razor-toothed mandibles. In files of hundreds of thousands, they stream into underground nests carrying their leaf pieces above their heads like parasols. Their underground colony may be home to more than a million leaf-cutter ants of various types and sizes. Inside the nest, the ants cut up the leaf pieces, chew them, and use them as food for a particular fungus that is the only food source for the leaf-cutters' larvae.

Prominent in horror movies about the jungle are the army ants, of which more than 240 species exist. Some of them travel in columns of as many as 20 million ants, columns that may be only a foot (30 centimeters) wide but several city blocks long. During the day, they may fan out across the rainforest floor, flushing out and eating scorpions, millipedes, katydids, and cockroaches. They climb into the nests of termites, wasps, and other ant species to plunder and eat their young. At night, army ants form living bivouacs with their own bodies to protect their queen and larvae.

Some tribal people who live in rainforests welcome the arrival of a column of army ants, because the ants enter

A line of army ants

their houses and eat cockroaches and other unwanted bugs before moving on through the forest. But other people force the advancing army to change directions by brushing the front of the column with feather fans and convincing the ants in the lead to march away from their houses.

The total weight of all the ants in a tropical rainforest may exceed the weight of all other noninsect animals, despite the ants' small size. Say tropical ecologists Adrian Forsyth and Ken Miyata, "No matter where you step, no matter where you lean, no matter where you sit, you will encounter ants."[4]

CONNECTIONS

The layers of the tropical rainforest are one of the main reasons for its incredible diversity. Each layer provides huge numbers of small, separate habitats for plants and animals. But not all the animals and plants of the rainforest live in only one or another of the forest's different layers. Some species connect the layers physically; others connect them in the way they feed or reproduce.

For example, climbing plants such as vines and the larger, woody vines called *lianas* stretch from the forest floor to the canopy. They are superimposed on the layers of the forest, occupying all levels. Climbers depend on rainforest trees to support them, but they have their own root structure in the soil.

Vines and lianas begin their lives as seeds on the forest floor. The seeds may have been dropped there by a bird or bat that has eaten the fruit of a mature vine. As it grows, the young vine encounters a tree, which it begins to climb, and heads up toward the light of the canopy. Once it reaches the sun, it matures, flowers, and bears fruit that will be eaten by animals and cast to the forest floor for germination.

Lianas not only connect the layers of the rainforest, but also connect the crowns of trees in the canopy. Because lianas are supported by other plants, they dedicate their energy to length and speed of growth. Some lianas grow to 3,000 feet (more than 900 meters). They may rise into one tree, loop down to the ground, and climb up a second tree for support. Gradually, these climbers link together the branches of several trees, sometimes with disastrous results for the trees. If one tree should fall, the connecting lianas may pull several other trees down with it.

EPIPHYTES EVERYWHERE

Like climbing vines and lianas, *epiphytes* make their homes on the surfaces of other plants. But there is one crucial difference. Epiphytes do not root in the soil, and they do not harm their hosts.

The name epiphyte derives from *epi*, meaning "upon," and *phyton*, which means "plant." Epiphytes are plants that depend on other plants for support and anchorage, rather than for nutrients. Epiphytes are not parasites on the host tree but are simply along for the ride. They live on nitrogen, minerals, and other nutrients brought to them in dripping water and dust. The "soil" that epiphytes live on is really the humus from the dead remains of other plants.

Epiphytes grow everywhere and in all layers of the rainforest—in full sun on the branches of canopy trees, on tree trunks in the understory, even on the dark forest floor. There are more than fifty thousand species of epiphytes in the world's rainforests. These include simple plants like mosses, lichens, and liverworts, and higher plants such as ferns, bromeliads, cacti, and orchids. But orchids are the epiphyte's true calling. There are at least twenty thousand species of rainforest orchids. Each has two sets of roots— thick, white ones that spread over the bark of the supporting tree and other, longer roots that absorb water and nutrients from the air, the ground, and from tree branches and trunks.[5]

Trees are sometimes lucky that the epiphytes are there.

Scientists once thought that epiphytes neither harmed nor helped their host trees. But they are now learning that epiphytes may help trees feed themselves. Because epiphytes increase the humidity of the tropical rainforest canopy, they make it easier for trees to absorb nitrogen from the air. And nitrogen is the tree's major food.

But epiphytes can be too successful. They sometimes grow so densely on tree limbs that the limbs break, and both limb and epiphytes crash to the tropical rainforest floor to be decomposed by insects and fungi.

Epiphytes are important to rainforest wildlife because they provide hiding places and breeding sites for many animals, especially frogs and insects. Tree-dwelling ants create nests in the root systems of epiphytes, and the bits and pieces of leaves and soil they bring into their nests serve as food for the epiphyte in return.

Epiphytes called bromeliads capture gallons of water in "tanks" made of upturned leaves. These reservoirs of water, held high in the forest canopy, provide habitat for salamanders, frogs, insects, and birds. High above the forest floor, holding on to the limbs of their host tree, epiphytes create a new habitat that specializes in animal life.

PARTNERS IN THE RAINFOREST

Finally, some plants and animals have become partners in the rainforest, and their life cycles overlap to connect the layers of the forest and the diversity they contain. For example, you may have eaten Brazil nuts, the tasty, hard-shelled nuts frequently served during the Christmas holiday

Epiphytes like this one grow everywhere in all layers of a tropical rainforest.

season. Brazil nuts grow in South America inside urn-shaped fruits on a jungle tree (*Bertholletia excelsa*) 150 feet (46 meters) tall. Forest Indians and rural families gather them from trees scattered throughout the forest. The United States imports $16 million worth of Brazil nuts every year.

But this lively industry depends on the activities of other rainforest species. Brazil nuts depend on bees for pollination and on rabbit-sized rodents, agoutis, for germination. Agoutis are the only animals that crack open the hard fruit case that contains the scores of Brazil nuts we recognize as food. The agoutis free the inner seeds from their hard-shelled home, allowing them to grow into more Brazil nut trees. Without either one of these links in the Brazil nuts' life cycle, there would be no Brazil nut trees.[6]

The story of the Brazil nut, bee, and agouti is only one of thousands that illustrates the wealth of wild species found in the tropical rainforest.

3
The Importance of Tropical Rainforests

The fate of tropical forests will be the major factor that determines the biological wealth of Earth in the future. Those extraordinarily vulnerable ecosystems are the greatest single reservoir of biotic diversity on the planet.

Paul and Anne Ehrlich, Stanford University

In our modern society of airplanes, microwave ovens, and plastic credit cards, it surprises us to learn that parts of our lives depend on tropical rainforests. But some of our basic foods, raw materials, and medicines come from these forests. The survival and future development of these important products depend upon protecting the rainforest ecosystem where they originated.

If you've ever eaten chocolate, a banana, a pineapple, or an avocado, you've already enjoyed food that originated in the rainforest. Today, our planet's rainforests protect the original genetic material, the *germ plasm*, that represents the potential of these foods to change. Germ plasm consists of combinations of genes, microscopic chemical messages of heredity that contain the biological instructions for building every part and characteristic of every living thing. Scientists and plant breeders use the genes in wild germ plasm to improve crops for our benefit.

Of the thousands of plant species used as food around the world, only a few hundred have been domesticated, meaning that people have altered their genetic structure to improve yields, increase their size, or in some way suit human purposes. Around thirty of these domesticated food plants provide 95 percent of the calories and protein that the world's population lives on, and several of the most important food plants originally came from tropical forests.

Because we depend on so few species of food plants, scientists must return periodically to these crops' wild ancestors in the rainforest to obtain fresh germ plasm. They use this germ plasm to create new varieties of our important food crops. They mix the wild varieties of these crops with domesticated varieties to produce strains that can survive plant diseases and insect plagues. Sometimes, introducing fresh germ plasm from ancestral plants is the only way to protect domesticated food crops from epidemic diseases. Because tropical rainforests are the original home of so many of these food plants, scientists seek to preserve these forests in order to preserve the wild varieties of our food crops.[1]

The most widely grown food crops from tropical rainforests are rice, corn, sweet potatoes, manioc (tapioca), sugarcane, bananas, oranges, and coffee. Other well-

Top: *coffee beans, Brazil nuts, vanilla, and cinnamon are tropical rainforest crops.*
Bottom: *you may find some of the more common forms of these crops in your kitchen.*

known tropical rainforest crops are mung beans, guavas, mangoes, papaya, pineapple, peanuts, cinnamon, cardomom, cloves, and pigeon peas.[2]

Rainforests have also provided some of the basic foods that we associate with particular countries. Without tropical rainforests, the Swiss would have no chocolate, the French would have no vanilla, and the Italians would have no tomato sauce. All these crops—cacao for chocolate, vanilla, and tomatoes—originated in tropical rainforests; in fact, in the tropical rainforests of Latin America. Chocolate, vanilla, and tomatoes were taken to Europe by early explorers who visited the New World and found these foods being eaten by Native Americans.

One of these New World crops, vanilla, is used in vanilla ice cream and in many pastries and candies. Vanilla had its origin in the rainforests of Mexico and Central America, where it grows as a wild vine up to 80 feet (24 meters) long. The Spanish explorer Hernán Cortés took vanilla beans back to Europe from Latin America in 1520, and vanilla quickly became a favorite flavoring for beverages and tobacco.

But European farmers' attempts to produce vanilla proved unsuccessful. The vanilla vines would grow, but they would not bear fruit. More than three hundred years passed before botanists discovered that the vanilla orchid is pollinated by a specific bee and by one type of hummingbird that live in tropical rainforests. Cortés had taken the vanilla vine from the rainforest, but he had left the plant's pollinators behind.[3]

In the modern world, some people have proposed that new developments in biotechnology (technology applied to biological or living organisms) will enable us to create whatever new plants we need. But they forget that biotechnology does not *create* genes or germ plasm; it merely *rearranges* them. In order to create new combinations of plant or animal genes, biotechnology depends on the original source material, the germ plasm held in existing plants and animals. So even new products created by scientists may depend on the ancient plants and animals of the tropical rainforest.

THE CASE OF TAPIOCA

Just one of these plants, manioc, is the food staple for 300 million people, most of whom live in Africa and Brazil. Although most Americans know manioc only in the form of tapioca pudding, manioc is one of the thirteen major food plants of the world. It grows as a shrubby tree 9 to 15 feet (3 to 5 meters) tall and produces roots that swell to be 1 to 2 feet long and 2 to 6 inches across (30 to 60 centimeters by 5 to 15 centimeters). Manioc roots can be boiled, pulverized to make flour, or even fermented and drunk as manioc beer. More than 440 *billion* pounds (200 million metric tons) of manioc are grown each year on 40,000 square miles (100,000 square kilometers) of tropical land.[4]

The plants that led to domesticated manioc still exist in the tropical rainforests of South America, and the world is fortunate that they do. During the 1930s, a virus called African mosaic disease struck the farmed varieties of manioc and threatened to destroy the major food source of millions of people. Plant scientists traveled to the rainforest of Amazonia to find the plant's wild predecessors. There, they collected varieties of manioc that were resistant to the virus. Through their efforts, manioc was saved.

BREAKFAST FROM THE RAINFOREST

The manioc story is only one example of how the genetic diversity of tropical rainforests protects human food supplies. Genetic resources from tropical rainforests have also saved bananas, sugarcane, cacao, and coffee.[5]

The root of the manioc plant (pictured here) is an important food source for millions of people in tropical forests in Africa and Latin America.

These forms of manioc were found in a West Indian
store in Brooklyn, New York: cassava (manioc)
bread, tapioca, and manioc root.

You may recognize some of these crops as breakfast foods. If you enjoy coffee, remember that coffee originated in the understory of the mountainous tropical forests of Ethiopia. Its wild precursors still grow there.

Or perhaps you like to drink hot chocolate and chocolate milk. Chocolate is made from cocoa, the ground beans of the cacao plant, which originated in the rainforest of the Amazon Basin in South America. Or maybe you enjoy a cup of hot tea in winter or a glass of iced tea on a hot summer day. Tea originally came from the rainforests of Southeast Asia.

Many of our favorite breakfast fruits also developed in tropical rainforests. Bananas, oranges, grapefruit, and pineapples originated in the forests of Southeast Asia. Papaya grew in the rainforests of Amazonia before Native American people brought it into their gardens. Sugarcane, the plant we use for making much of our white and brown sugar, grows wild in the tropical rainforests of Indonesia.

As ethnobotanist Mark Plotkin of the World Wildlife Fund–U.S. points out, "Each and every one of us is eating tropical rainforests for breakfast."

NEW FOODS FROM THE FOREST

Among the thousands of undescribed species of plants that grow in the world's tropical rainforests, no doubt a number of plants could serve as new foods. A few that have been promoted as new fruits are the feijoa (*Feijoa sellowiana*),

Now the most common fruit eaten in the United States, the banana originated in the tropical rainforests of Southeast Asia. Note that bananas grow "upside down" on the plant.

(50)

*Assorted tropical fruits of the
Annona family which may one
day be common in your supermarket.
The photograph came from the
Fruit and Spice Park in
Homestead, Dade County, Florida.*

a pineapple-flavored relative of the guava from tropical South America; the rambutan (*Nephelium lappaceum*) from tropical Southeast Asia; and the naranjilla (*Solanum quitoense*), which looks like a furry tomato but tastes like a strawberry/pineapple. In Ecuador, some families already drink naranjilla juice instead of orange juice for breakfast.

You may already have tried kiwi, a fuzzy, egg-shaped fruit that came from the tropical forests of southern China, where it was known as Chinese gooseberry. Once known only in those forests, kiwis are now cultivated on sprawling plantations in California and New Zealand.

Before you reject the idea that we might soon be eating new tropical rainforest crops, keep in mind that a century ago bananas were considered an exotic food. When they were first introduced to United States consumers more than a hundred years ago, bananas were sold individually wrapped, and they cost two dollars each.

Keep in mind also that twenty years ago, the average U.S. supermarket carried only 65 different fruits and vegetables in its fresh produce section. Today, many supermarkets have at least 140 species, and some have 250. In Florida, where many tropical food crops are grown for the first time in the United States, one supermarket sells more than 400 different fruits and vegetables during the course of the year.[6]

MEDICINES FROM THE JUNGLE

Tropical forests are also a prime source of new medicines. When you visit your local pharmacy, chances are one in four that the prescription the pharmacist hands you is derived from a plant. Chances are one in four or five that the original ingredients came from a tropical rainforest; for example, hydrocortisone used to treat inflammation, quinine for malaria, and ipecac to cause vomiting in case of poisoning.

Tropical rainforests have given us drugs that show promise in the treatment of cancer, sickle-cell anemia, Parkinson's disease, hypertension, and heart disease. When U.S. botanist Monie S. Hudson examined fifteen hundred rainforest plants he had gathered in Costa Rica, he found that 15 percent carried potential in the campaign against cancer. Physicians are well aware of the rainforest's future as a source of new medications. Officials of the U.S. National Cancer Institute have said that destroying tropical rainforests would cause a major setback to their search for anticancer drugs.[7]

In short, the world's tropical rainforests are an almost unlimited chemical factory waiting for the attention of scientific research. We'll take another look at this benefit in chapter 4, because most of the rainforest medicines we use were shown to us by tribal people who live in the tropical rainforest.

OTHER RAINFOREST PRODUCTS

Tropical rainforests are also the source of many raw products that we use everyday. Tropical wood is probably the best example. Most Americans have sat on furniture made from trees from the tropical rainforest. Mahogany from Central America is one of the finest woods known for making furniture and office paneling. Teak wood from Southeast Asia has been used in shipbuilding for centuries. Even the balsa wood used to make model airplanes comes from a tropical rainforest tree.

Tropical rainforests also provide a variety of other valuable natural products. Fibers, latexes, resins, waxes, acids, alcohols, flavorings, sweeteners, and dyes are just a few of the raw materials we find there. If you've ever worn a life jacket while water-skiing or riding in a boat, you've had the fiber of the kapok tree on your back. Because it is waterproof and isn't attacked by insects, kapok is used for lifesaving equipment and insulation. Kapok is the silky floss found in the seed pods of the ceiba tree, which grows in the rainforests of Africa, Southeast Asia, and tropical Latin America.

Another popular rainforest fiber comes from the toquilla plant, which grows in the rainforests of Central and South America. Hat makers in Ecuador split toquilla fibers to make fine white hats called Panama hats because they first became popular among men building the Panana Canal.

You may even have found yourself in trouble for chewing rainforest latex during class. The natural base for chewing gum is the white latex of the sapodilla, or chicle, tree (*Achras zapota*), which grows in the rainforests of Central America. Men called chicleros search the forest for chicle trees and cut a hatched pattern on the trees' bark to allow

Three years after Calvin discovered these petroleum trees, Brazilian Indians led him to the copaiba tree (*Copaifera langsdorfii*), which produces almost pure diesel fuel like that burned by large trucks. Calvin learned that Indian families drill a small hole in the tree's 3-foot-(9-meter-) thick trunk and force a plug into it. Then, twice a year, they return to the tree, remove the plug, and take out 15 to 20 quarts (14 to 19 liters) of liquid hydrocarbons. The Indians use the oil as a skin softener, but Calvin found that the liquid can be poured directly into the fuel tank of a diesel-powered car. He predicted that an acre (0.4 hectare) of one hundred mature trees could produce twenty-five barrels of fuel each year. That possibility now has researchers in Brazil and Okinawa planting experimental plantations of what may turn out to be the first commercial motor-fuel tree.[10]

JUNGLE BUG KILLERS

Another great promise of the rainforest is help in controlling pests that eat agricultural crops. Because rainforests have so many different plant species and an astronomical number of insects, many forest plants have evolved chemicals that repel insect pests. That means that natural insecticides are plentiful in the rainforest.

These natural chemicals have prompted researchers to search the rainforest for new types of insecticides that are less harmful to humans than the synthetic chemicals that farmers now use.

One such natural insecticide is obtained from the rainforest plants called derris, which grow as woody climbers (*lianas*) in Southeast Asia. The roots of derris lianas contain a group of toxic chemicals called rotenoids, which are used by rainforest tribes as fish poisons and poisons for the tips of arrows. But rotenoids from the rainforest can also be used to control insects that eat food crops, as well as insect pests such as house flies, moths, fleas, lice, and ticks.

Hundreds of other natural insecticides must lie undiscovered in the world's tropical rainforests. In southern Mexico, for example, the people of a rainforest tribe called the Lacandon Maya use the powdered bark and sticky sap of a tree they call tzayok (*Aspidosperma magalocarpon*) to kill cockroaches. They use beams cut from the tree to build houses. The beams control cockroaches by releasing chemicals that are harmless to human beings but deadly to roaches. The Indians also daub the sap of the tree on ropes they use to hang fruit and meat from their house rafters. Roaches will climb down the ropes, trying to get to the food, but fall off the rope and die when they touch the tzayok sap.

Rainforest insects can also fight insects that eat farmers' crops. Before 1910, the sugarcane beetle borer plagued sugarcane plantations in Hawaii and cost farmers almost $1 million a year because of the crops they destroyed. But that year, researchers found a parasite that kills the beetle— the tachinid fly that lives in the tropical rainforest of New Guinea. When they brought the fly to Hawaii, it began to feed on the beetle, saving farmers great sums of money.[11]

CLOUDS, RAIN, FLOODS, AND SOIL

Tropical rainforests also provide important services simply because they exist. For example, rainforests act like a giant sponge. A sudden cloudburst in a tropical forest may drop an inch (2.5 centimeters) of rain in half an hour. That's forty times more water than the average rain shower in Boston or Washington, D.C. More than half the rain that hits the rainforest is intercepted by the canopy. The forest soaks up the rain that falls on it and releases it gradually into streams and rivers. It recycles much of the rest back

into the atmosphere through evaporation. What water remains trickles down the leaves and stems of rainforest plants to drip into the thin soil and into the plants of the understory.

The rain that evaporates from the rainforest vegetation may fall on it again during the next rain shower. For rainforests do exactly what their name implies—they make rain. Studies in Panama and in the Amazon show that over half the rain that falls on a tropical rainforest is water recycled by the forest itself. The leaves of forest vegetation breathe out water vapor equal to thousands of gallons of water per acre per day. This water vapor combines with evaporated water from the oceans to create rain.

If the rainforest is cleared, that recycling system is destroyed, and the amount of rainfall can be cut in half. In central Panama, where most of the rainforest has been cut down to create cattle ranches, the amount of rain that falls each year has dropped by 17 inches (43 centimeters) in fifty years. Because less water is rising into the air in vapor form, less is returning in the form of rain.[12]

Tropical rainforests also capture precipitation from clouds and fog and add it to the ecosystem. Removing this forest can lower groundwater levels and decrease the amount of water in wells and natural springs.

Rainforests can also help prevent floods. Because they absorb rainfall, they hold water, releasing it gradually for the benefit of farmers and cities downstream. If the forest is removed, heavy rains quickly run off the barren land-

Mist rises from a tropical
rainforest in Guatemala.
Rainforests recycle the water
that falls on them; clearing
them can decrease the
rainfall in the area.

scape, causing unpredictable flooding and choking rivers and streams with eroded soil.

If a region's rainfall disappears in flash floods, little water is left to support agriculture and the needs of human beings. Some cities in tropical countries are protecting nearby rainforests to preserve their supply of water. Tegucigalpa, the capital city of Honduras, protects the nearby forest of Los Laureles to guarantee that the city has enough water for its citizens.

Eradicating rainforests also causes soil erosion. When tropical forests are cleared, rain hits the exposed soil, and the water rushes off the land carrying the soil with it. Because the rainforest protects the soil from rain and runoff, 2.5 acres (1 hectare) of forest will lose only 2 pounds (1 kilogram) of topsoil per year due to erosion. But if the forest is cleared, those same 2.5. acres (a hectare) of land may lose 68,000 pounds (31 metric tons) of topsoil.[13]

As that topsoil washes downstream, it smothers fish and wipes out farmers' crops by covering them with silt. If soil erosion is severe enough, the soil can fill up the reservoirs of hydroelectric dams and ruin their ability to produce electricity.

Siltation caused by forest clearing around the Panama Canal is now 22 feet (6.7 meters) deep in Lake Alajuela, one of the lakes that supplies fresh water to the canal's locks and allows ships to float through. Some researchers say that siltation is so severe that by the time the canal is fully transferred to the country of Panama in 1999, it may have become a worthless ditch.[14]

Another of the possible repercussions of tropical deforestation would affect human beings everywhere. Some scientists claim that worldwide destruction of tropical rainforests may contribute to changing the global climate. The level of carbon dioxide in the earth's atmosphere is increasing, and it seems clear that eradicating tropical rainforests is partly responsible for this. Burning tropical rainforests, like burning fossil fuels, releases carbon dioxide into the atmosphere. This carbon dioxide absorbs part of the sun's energy that normally bounces back into space. As more heat is absorbed by the increasing level of carbon dioxide, it warms the surface of the planet through a process that scientists call "the greenhouse effect."

If some scientists' predictions come true, the increasing concentration of atmospheric carbon dioxide may raise the average global temperature by about 1 degree centigrade (1.8 degrees Fahrenheit) by the year A.D. 2000 and by 2 degrees centigrade (3.6 degrees Fahrenheit) within seventy years. One possible result of this trend will be changes in rainfall that could seriously affect crop production. Another possibility is a rise of up to 20 feet (6 meters) in the world's sea levels. This increase in sea levels could come if the polar ice caps melted and began to slide off the geological formations that support them. Such an increase would flood major parts of Florida, for example, and would flood coastal cities around the world. If we consider that 40 percent of the world's population lives on the coastline, the repercussions of such an event are alarming.[15]

While some scientists doubt that the oceans will rise enough to flood coastal cities, none now doubt that an increase in atmospheric carbon dioxide is occurring. And all scientists agree that this increase will have serious implications for human society.

MIGRATING SPECIES

It is also important to remember that tropical rainforests are not only the full-time habitat of millions of tropical species, but also the part-time home of some animals we think of as "ours" in the temperate world.

For example, tropical rainforests are the winter home for thousands of kinds of birds that migrate south every year from the United States and Canada. Many of the birds that we feed as backyard residents—warblers, tanagers, thrushes, and orioles—spend much of each year in the tropical rainforests of Latin America. Of the 650 species of birds that breed in the United States, more than one-third pass their winters in the Latin American tropics.[16]

Taken together, the animals, plants, and services of the tropical rainforest remind us that these forests have played a vital role in the evolution of life on earth. They also show us that rainforests continue to make important contributions to the future of human life.

4
People of the Tropical Rainforest

In the jungle, the Indian knows everything.

Proverb from the
country of Suriname,
South America

A LIFETIME IN THE FOREST

Michu is about as happy as a teenager can be. After a day spent hunting in the forest with his father and older brother, he's headed down the trail toward the lake behind his house. At the shore, he slips into a long canoe his father and grandfather carved from a giant mahogany tree. He paddles far out into the water to watch the sunset shimmer over Lake Tz'ibatnah, named for the rain god whose bones are hidden in a nearby cave.

Michu takes off his long, white tunic and leaps from the boat into the coolness of the water. The splash frightens

*Michu Valenzuela, a Lacandon Maya Indian, paddles
a mahogany canoe across Lake Tz'ibatnah
in the rainforest of Chiapas, Mexico.*

half a dozen long-legged shore birds, and they slowly lift themselves into the air. In the rainforest, a troupe of howler monkeys calls out a protest at being disturbed.

Surveying the scene, Michu declares the day a total success. But he still keeps a sharp eye out for crocodiles.

Michu is one of four hundred Lacandon Maya Indians who live in the tropical rainforest of southeastern Mexico. He has lived in the forest all his life, hunting, fishing, and eating wild fruit and food from his family's garden. He does not know how old he is by our calendar. Lacandones have no need for birth certificates. He may be fourteen or fifteen.

The rainforest is his school, and his relatives—his father and mother, uncles, older brothers, and grandmothers—are his teachers. They teach him what he needs to know to survive in the tropical forest. They teach him how to hunt deer and wild forest pigs called peccaries, how to grow corn and squash, and how to build a house of poles and palm leaves. They teach him the sounds of the forest animals and the names of jungle plants that cure sickness. Though he knows a great deal by the time he is a teenager, this education will continue all his life.

When his beard begins to appear, he will hike an hour through the rainforest to the thatch house of the girl he hopes to marry. He will sit on the dirt floor with the girl's father and smoke strong cigars from tobacco grown in his forest garden plot. Nervously, he will ask the man for the hand of his daughter in marriage. If both the girl and the father agree, Michu and the girl will sit together and eat a meal of beans and tortillas, signifying that they are now married.

With the passing years, Michu and his wife will bear children of their own. And they will teach them about the rainforest, as they themselves were taught. And as long as the forest survives, they will be part of a heritage of knowledge passed down, generation to generation, through centuries of living with the rainforest.

The collared peccary is often
hunted by rainforest peoples.

A WORLD OF TROPICAL RAINFOREST PEOPLE

Tribal people like the Lacandon Maya live throughout the world's tropical rainforests—in Latin America, Asia, and Africa. They are part of more than 200 million people who live within the planet's rainforests. Many of these families are recent immigrants to the forest. They have migrated into the rainforest from other regions of their countries. But for centuries before the immigrants began to arrive, the only people in the rainforest were tribal peoples like the Lacandon Maya.

The people of tropical rainforest tribes understand that their lives are based on the forest ecosystem that surrounds them. From the incredible diversity of the rainforest, they gather edible fruit, wild animals for protein, fiber for clothing and ropes, incense for religious ceremonies, natural insecticides, fish poisons, wood for houses, furniture, and canoes, and medicinal plants that may cure a toothache or a snakebite.

Their understanding of the plants and animals of the tropical rainforest is unequaled even by teams of modern scientists. Because tribal people have lived in the rainforest for thousands of years, they have had the time it takes to understand which plants and animals are useful and which they must avoid.

Through their remarkable understanding of the rainforest, tribal people have been able to show us an impressive collection of useful products from the forest. It was rainforest people who taught us to use chocolate, Brazil nuts, sweet potatoes, tobacco, avocados, vanilla, coffee, manioc, mangoes, papaya, peanuts, cinnamon, bananas, and sugarcane. Rainforest tribes showed us useful materials such as rubber and glues, gum arabic for ink, new medicines, latexes for chewing gum and golf balls, and natural insecticides. Rainforest tribes in South America have shown scientists 268 different plants that can be used to control human fertility.[1]

STUDYING TRIBAL PLANT USE

Some scientists dedicate their careers to learning more about the traditional knowledge of rainforest peoples. Dr. Mark Plotkin of the World Wildlife Fund—U.S. spends much of his time living with rainforest peoples to study how they use the plants of the jungle. Plotkin is an *ethnobotanist*, a scientist who studies the use of plants by tribal peoples. He works with traditional healers in Madagascar and with Indians in South America. Plotkin explores the forest with rainforest *shamans*, or tribal medicine men, to discover which plants the tribe uses as medicines, as poison for arrow points, and as fibers to make ropes and twines.

Describing this work, Plotkin says that "to the Indian who inhabits it, the tropical forest is a combination supermarket, pharmacy, hardware store, and sporting goods shop." Almost all the tribal people's daily needs, he says, are met by the plant and animal products they find in the tropical rainforest.[2]

MEDICINES FROM THE RAINFOREST

As Plotkin and other researchers have learned, tribal peoples have made especially good use of the chemical properties of rainforest plants. Rainforest tribes have discovered hundreds of plants that serve as medicines, and they have used them against illnesses for centuries.

Most of the medicines that physicians call "wonder drugs," such as reserpine for nervous disorders, vincristine for leukemia, and digitalis for heart failure, come from plants that were first used by tribal peoples. In fact, several of our most important medicines were shown to us in their raw forms by rainforest peoples.[3]

Some of these medicines came to us through the research of Dr. Richard Evans Schultes of Harvard University. Schultes studies ethnobotany among the Indians of the Amazon rainforest and has spent years living with different

*Dr. Mark Plotkin collects
medicinal plants with a
Yanomamo Indian medicine man.*

tribes. He has collected more than thirteen hundred plant species used by Indians of the northwest Amazon as medicines, poisons, or narcotics.[4]

Ethnobotanists like Schultes and Plotkin say that learning about medicinal plants from tribal peoples is important because there are far too many plants for scientists in laboratories to examine each one for curing properties. Of the five hundred thousand known species of living plants, only a fraction have been investigated in the laboratory. By focusing on plant species used by tribal people, researchers can take a valuable shortcut, because tribal people have had thousands of years of trial and error to discover which plants cure and which can kill.

One ethnobotanist, Dr. Brian Boom, of the New York Botanical Garden, marked off a 10-acre (4-hectare) plot of rainforest near a village of Chácobo Indians in Bolivia. He found ninety-one species of trees in the plot. To test all these tree species in a laboratory would have taken years. But Boom saved a great deal of effort and time by questioning the Chácobo Indians about their use of the trees he found. The Indians answered that they use seventy-five of the ninety-one tree species as medicines, food, or fibers.[5]

On the other side of the world, the Gayo hill tribe people of Sumatra (Indonesia) use more than 170 medicinal plants to cure illnesses from kidney problems to measles. Here's one example from a single species: the tribal people use the raw seeds of one rainforest tree (*Parkia roxburghii*) to relieve headaches. Roasted and mashed, the seeds cure colic, a disorder that causes great discomfort in babies. The seeds also kill parasitic worms and will help cuts heal rapidly.[6]

FROM ARROW POISON TO SURGERY

One important drug that we use today in heart surgery was discovered in use among rainforest peoples as a poison for the tips of arrows. Early explorers in South American rainforests found that Indians of the region prepare a sticky black substance, curare, from the resin of a jungle liana, *Chondodendron tomentosum*. The Indians apply this substance to the tips of their arrows. If a treated arrow pierces the skin of an animal, it paralyzes the creature's central nervous system. The Indians' use of curare makes the difficult task of hunting in the rainforest easier.

Today, alkaloids from this climbing vine are injected into patients undergoing heart or abdominal surgery to relax the body's muscles and allow the surgeon to work. The same drug is also used to treat spasms caused by tetanus and some forms of paralysis. Because chemists have not been able to produce a synthetic version of curare that retains all the actions of the natural product, they continue to rely on alkaloids extracted from wild plants.[7]

JUNGLE BIRTH CONTROL PILLS

A similar story concerns the yam of the Mexican barbasco (*Dioscorea composita*), another rainforest climbing vine. Forty years ago, the barbasco vine was known only as a jungle fish poison used by Indians to stun fish in rivers. The Indians pound the yams into a pulp, then pour them in the river. Any fish that the substance reaches becomes paralyzed. They float to the surface, and the Indians collect them for food.

In the 1930s, a chemistry professor named Russell Marker gathered the barbasco vine in the rainforest of southeastern Mexico. He took the plants back to his laboratory in Chicago, where he isolated a chemical compound called diosgenin. Diosgenin became the active ingredient in oral contraceptives—birth control pills. Today, around the world, millions of women take oral contraceptives, and the barbasco vine has become the basis for a prosperous industry in Mexico. Diosgenin from the

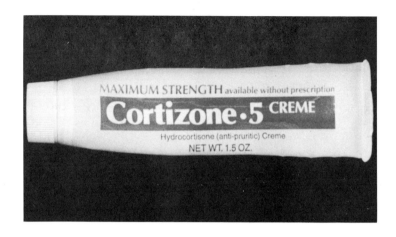

*Cortisone is produced
from a rainforest vine.*

same rainforest vine is also used to produce cortisone (hydrocortisone) for the treatment of rheumatoid arthritis, rheumatic fever, and inflammation of the skin and eyes.[8]

CURES FOR CANCER IN THE RAINFOREST

During the 1960s, children with leukemia, Hodgkin's disease, and other cancers had a 20 percent chance of long-term survival. Today, children with these diseases have an 80 percent chance of surviving for many years. The difference is the development of two new drugs from the rosy periwinkle (*Catharanthus roseus*), a plant that grows in dry tropical forests in Madagascar.

Over eighty *alkaloids* (organic compounds that contain nitrogen) have been extracted from the rosy periwinkle, and six of them have antitumor properties. When it was discovered, the rosy periwinkle was being used by traditional curers as a treatment for diabetes.

In his book on endangered species, *The Sinking Ark*, Norman Myers points out that 70 percent of the plants known to have anticancer properties come from lowland tropical forests. Most of these plants are used by rainforest peoples for the treatment of illnesses.

HUNTERS AND GATHERERS

Traditional tribal people, living in tropical rainforests around the world, have learned how to use the rainforest to provide food for their families. Some groups, like the BaMbuti Pygmies of West Africa, do not grow food, but instead gather it wild from the forest.

The BaMbuti Pygmies live in the Ituri rainforest in the countries of Zaire and the Congo in West Africa. They are some of the smallest people in the world. The men stand only 4.5 feet (1.4 meters) tall, and woman may be 2 inches (5 centimeters) shorter.

But the pygmies' size is of benefit to them in the rainforest. Being small allows them to hike quickly through the forest to follow game animals. Their size also helps them cast off the heat of the jungle from their bodies, because they have little bulk but a large area of exposed skin that radiates heat.

The BaMbuti Pygmies live in bands of related families. Each band—made up of twenty to one hundred people—lives together and hunts together. They also gather fruits, berries, palm shoots, nuts, and honey in the rainforest. For hunting, the BaMbuti use bows and arrows to kill monkeys and other mammals such as antelope and rodents. Some bands cooperate in teams to drive animals into nets made from jungle vines. Women and children march through the rainforest pounding on wood drums and tree trunks to scare animals toward a semicircle of men holding nets and wood spears. When the animals run into the nets, the men move forward to kill them with spears coated with plant poisons.

When the hunt is over, the band returns to cook the meat in their huts built from tree saplings and leaves. By wisely harvesting the bounty of the tropical rainforest, BaMbuti Pygmies have plenty of food and plenty of free time to spend as a family, telling stories and singing songs of the hunt and of life in the forest.

Anthropologist Colin Turnbull, from the American Museum of Natural History in New York City, lived several years with the BaMbuti Pygmies and published a fascinating book about their lives, *The Forest People*.

FARMERS IN THE RAINFOREST

In southeastern Mexico, Michu's tribe, the Lacandon Maya, spend part of their time hunting monkeys, tiny brocket deer, and large, tasty rodents called pacas. Until the 1950s, Lacandon hunters used long bows and arrows tipped with flint or a black, volcanic stone called obsidian. Today, the Lacandones hunt with .22-caliber rifles, using ammunition purchased in towns outside the rainforest.

The Lacandones also gather wild plants in the forest: palm hearts from spined palm trees in the understory, sweet pulp from the seed pods of jungle trees, and climbing lianas that can be boiled to make a refreshing drink that tastes like strawberry soda. Another liana serves as a jungle canteen. If a hunter gets thirsty traveling through the forest, he can cut a section from a hanging yuhi vine (*Vitis tilifolia*) for a quick drink of pure water.

But unlike the BaMbuti Pygmies, the Lacandon Maya (as well as many other rainforest peoples) are primarily

A Lacandon Maya boy strips the cover from an edible palm heart in the Chiapas rainforest.

farmers. They have learned to grow food in the infertile tropical soils by using special agricultural techniques.

The Lacandones create garden plots by clearing the rainforest from an area around 2.5 acres (1 hectare) in size. They cut the undergrowth first to create a clear space in which to cut down the large trees. They let the cleared vegetation dry for a month or more, then burn it in huge fires. They are careful to avoid setting the surrounding jungle on fire by cutting firebreaks—wide clearings without combustible vegetation. If the nearby forest were burned, too many weeds would sprout in the garden.

By burning the dried leaves and felled tree trunks, the Lacandones create a temporarily fertile soil by turning the nutrients captured in the vegetation into ash. Then they quickly plant the area with fast-growing tree crops and root crops like bananas and sweet potatoes. These crops begin to absorb the nutrients in the ash, preventing them from being washed away when the spring rains begin.

After the first crops take hold, the farmer and his family go on to plant dozens of other crops—corn, onions, garlic, pineapples, watermelons, limes, grapefruit, squash, beans, cotton, tomatoes, mint, tobacco, rice, plums, sugarcane, ginger, and cacao.

They know when to plant these crops by watching the rainforest around them. When the flowers of the mahogany tree fall in the forest, the farmer knows that it is time to plant corn. The falling of the flowers of the corkwood tree indicates the days to plant watermelons. Instead of relying on a calendar that is the same year after year, Lacandon farmers time their crops to the actual conditions of the rainforest they live in.

After five to seven years of harvesting the garden plot, the farmer plants the area in trees like rubber, avocado,

Michu drinking from a rainforest water vine

Left: a *Lacandon Maya* man surveys the burned
vegetation of a cleared rainforest plot.
He will now plant the area in food crops
in anticipation of the spring rains.
Above: a *Lacandon Maya* man stands in his garden
plot, surrounded by corn and sweet potato vines.

and oranges and clears another garden for corn and other crops. As the old garden plot regenerates with natural forest species, the farmer continues to harvest the tree crops for many years. When the forest finally overtakes the tree crops and heals itself into rainforest, the farmer will once again cut and burn the area for corn.

Under this system of rainforest farming, the forest becomes a garden, which becomes an orchard, which becomes rainforest once again, and so on through time. By recycling forest and garden in this fashion, Lacandon farmers destroy very little rainforest. Instead, they use the forest's resources to feed, clothe, and house themselves in harmony with their jungle home.

IMMIGRANTS IN
THE TROPICAL RAINFOREST

During the past twenty-five years, millions of people have moved into tropical rainforests from other ecosystems in other parts of their countries. In South America, farm families are moving into the lowland rainforests of Colombia, Ecuador, and Peru. In Brazil, poor farmers from the dry areas of Brazil's eastern coast are migrating into the Amazon. Similar patterns of migration are taking place in the tropical regions of Africa and Southeast Asia.

In a government program called transmigration, Indonesian settlers from the crowded Southeast Asian islands of Bali and Java are moving into the rainforests of Indonesia's outer islands—Sumatra, Sulawesti, Kalimantan (part of Borneo), and Irian Jaya (the western half of the island of New Guinea).

The Indonesian government has promised to create new farms for the settlers by clearing rainforests and draining swamps. Government programs give the colonists 5 acres (2 hectares) of free land, seeds and tools, and free

Indonesian transmigrants walk into newly cleared land on the west coast of South Sumatra. Indonesia is airlifting millions of people from the crowded islands of Java, Bali, and Madura to sparsely populated islands such as South Sumatra.

food for the first year and a half. From that point forward, the families are expected to farm the tropical soils and survive on their own.

But doing so is difficult. Environmental writer Catherine Caufield visited the Indonesian transmigration project as part of the research for her book *In the Rainforest*. She learned that the rainforests of parts of Sumatra and Sulawesi are being destroyed and that the soils are eroding as quickly as they are cleared. Settlers are clashing with tribal peoples who have lived in the forest for centuries. Elephants and tigers have lost so much of their habitat that they raid the settlers' farms, destroying plants and killing livestock.

But still the program is continuing. The government has moved 1.5 million people to the outer islands and plans to move 3 million more. Caufield writes that "what keeps transmigration going is that there are plenty of people who want land so badly that they are willing to endure the hardships of pioneering to get it." But, she continues, if the land is not protected, the people's hopes will be short-lived.[9]

HARDSHIPS IN THE JUNGLE

As the Indonesian transmigration program indicates, living in the tropical rainforest is not an adventure in an amusement park. Up to half of all babies born in some rainforest regions die before the age of one. As teenagers and adults, rainforest people are threatened by a variety of diseases and accidents. Malaria and yellow fever, diseases spread by mosquito bites, kill many. Falls from trees, snakebites, and homicides are serious dangers. And diseases like measles and chicken pox, which are rarely fatal to people from the developed world, can be deadly to tribal people with no previous exposure to these diseases and no vaccinations against them. Epidemics of measles still kill children and adults among many tropical rainforest tribes.

Many of these diseases have been introduced to rainforest peoples through contact with outsiders. Before they are contacted by explorers, road builders, or immigrant farm families, rainforest peoples are remarkably free of infectious diseases. But once new diseases are introduced, rainforest peoples quickly fall prey to them. And in many cases, families who settle on tropical rainforest land are victims of the same diseases.

DISAPPEARING KNOWLEDGE

The remarkable thing about tropical rainforest people is that some of them have been so successful. Centuries ago, rainforest peoples even developed cities in the jungle. In the tropical rainforest region of northwestern Kampuchea (Cambodia), the city of Angkor served as the royal center for a dynasty of Khmer kings. For more than five hundred years (during the ninth through the fourteenth centuries), Angkor was the capital city of one of the largest, most sophisticated kingdoms in the history of Southeast Asia. The city included complexes of religious temples, water reservoirs, and irrigation canals.

Several centuries earlier, in the New World, the Classic Maya built a civilization with mathematics, a written language, and a calendar more accurate than our own. Between A.D. 250 and A.D. 900, they lived in cities of a hundred thousand people or more in tropical rainforest areas now located in the countries of Mexico, Guatemala, Belize, and Honduras.

Angkor was eventually conquered by warriors from Thailand, and the city was abandoned during the 1400s. But why the Maya civilization disintegrated is a question that archeologists spend their entire careers trying to answer. We still don't know the answer. We are left only with the silent ruins of ancient cities in the rainforest— Tikal, Yaxchilán, Copán, and scores of others.

*The ruins of the Maya city of Tikal in the
rainforest of northern Guatemala*

Maya peoples still live today in Mexico, Belize, and Guatemala, but only a few groups remain in the tropical rainforest, where they preserve some elements of the Classic Maya's knowledge of the rainforest. You can learn more about the Classic Maya and their modern descendants in two well-illustrated books, *The Mysterious Maya*, by George Stuart and Gene Stuart, and *Lost Empires, Living Tribes* (both Washington D.C.: National Geographic Society, 1977 and 1982, respectively).

THE FUTURE OF
RAINFOREST PEOPLES

For thousands of years, the small populations of rainforest tribes and their skillful manner of harvesting the forest without destroying it allowed people and forest to coexist. Today, however, new people are entering the forest. Some, like the families in the Indonesian transmigration program, are looking for land and new lives. Others hope to plunder the valuable timber trees and animal life to be found in the rainforest. People who come into the jungle hoping to get rich quickly sometimes bring sophisticated machines and technology as their tools. But they lack the detailed understanding of the rainforest that tribal peoples have developed over hundreds of years.

We're only beginning to learn part of the information that rainforest peoples can share with us about their complex environment. But just when we are coming to appreciate their understanding of the forest, both the people and the forests are threatened with extinction. Unfortunately, the knowledge that has allowed rainforest tribes to survive in the tropical forest without destroying it is quickly disappearing. As the world's tropical rainforests are cleared and burned for agriculture and cattle ranching, for logging, and for colonization projects, humankind is losing the intricate knowledge of rainforest peoples.

Ethnobotanist Mark Plotkin makes the point clearly: "Forest peoples are dying out and their oral traditions are disappearing with them. Each time a medicine man dies, it is as if a library has burned down."

In the following chapter, we'll look at why tropical rainforests are being eradicated in many places around the world. With an understanding of why this is happening, we'll be better prepared in the future to prevent it.

5
Tropical Rainforests in Danger

It is up to science to spread the understanding that the choice is not between wild places or people. Rather, it is between a rich or an impoverished existence for Man.

Thomas E. Lovejoy,
World Wildlife Fund

Jacinto Trujillo worked hard for more than a month to clear the thick rainforest vegetation from his 2-acre (1-hectare) plot of land. After the rainy season stopped in November, Trujillo selected this spot as the most promising for next year's corn crop. In January, he began to clear the forest understory to give himself ample room to swing his axe as he began to fell the giant rainforest trees. Cutting hour after hour on every tree, Trujillo chopped until the trees began to creak, then finally crashed through the canopy with the roar of splintering wood.

With all the vegetaton cleared from the plot of land, Trujillo waited for more than a month while the sun dried the moisture from the dead trees, lianas, and palm trees. Finally, as April approached, he returned to the pile of dried vegetation and built small fires on three sides of it. The fires crackled as they built into a giant inferno of burning jungle. Animals that had hidden in fallen logs dashed from the flames toward the darkness of the surrounding forest. Flames leaped higher as more tree trunks caught fire, sending great plumes of smoke into the sky. There, it joined the smoke of fires burning in the plots of Trujillo's neighbors, all of them corn farmers like himself.

After the fire had died and the smoke had cleared, Trujillo and his wife and three sons returned to the scorched plot and began to poke holes in the ashes with a 6-foot (2-meter) pole called a dibble stick. Into each hole they dropped five kernels of corn. These were the seeds that would produce the year's corn crop and, with luck, carry Trujillo and his family through another year of life as colonists in the rainforest.

Around the world, this scene is played out on a gigantic scale every year. Millions of families like Trujillo's clear and burn small plots of tropical rainforest to plant food crops and crops to sell. Added together, these small plots add up to huge areas of jungle destroyed each year.

In simply trying to produce food for his family, Jacinto Trujillo and millions of farmers like him add to the growing problem of tropical rainforest destruction. It's important to point out that these families do not destroy tropical forests out of maliciousness or anger. They are merely trying to produce food and income for their families in the only way they know how. But combined with the other causes of tropical forest clearing, this destruction of the earth's rainforests is changing the face of the earth and eliminating many of the species of plants and animals that we share it with.

DEFORESTATION
AND SPECIES EXTINCTION

One hundred years from now, the decades that we are now living may be known as the brief period of history when one-fourth of the earth's plant and animal species were wiped out. Scientists speak of the end of the dinosaur age as a time of massive extinctions, but during those several million years the planet lost an average of only one species every thousand years.

Today, human beings are eradicating plants and animals at the rate of a *thousand* species per year. By the end of the twentieth century, this rate may reach ten thousand species destroyed each year, or more than one species eradicated every hour. Some scientists point out that predictions about the number of species being eradicated are nothing more than estimates. Because we don't even know how many species there are on earth, they say, how can we talk about how many species are being destroyed? At the same time, these scientists also admit that plants and animals are being rapidly decimated in many parts of the tropics, and they acknowledge that these extinctions will change the course of evolution.[1]

Why is this massive extinction of plant and animal species taking place? The most direct answer to that question is one simple phrase—destruction of habitat—or the eradication of the species' physical environment. But in most cases, that phrase can be narrowed down to one word, *deforestation*, the clearing and burning of the world's forests. Most of the species extinction we are seeing during the final decades of the twentieth century are caused by the destruction of tropical rainforests.

The reason that tropical rainforest destruction is so serious is simple. More species live in the rainforests than in any other ecosystem on earth. Destroying the world's rainforests means wiping out hundreds of thousands—perhaps millions—of kinds of plants and animals.

Most of the species eradicated by tropical deforestation are insects, chiefly beetles and butterflies. Insects are the most numerous creatures in the rainforest. But in addition to wiping out insect species, deforestation also exterminates a wealth of birds, mammals, and reptiles, and thousands of species of plants.

The ironic thing about this destruction is that we know so little about what we're destroying. Five out of six tropical species have never been seen by scientists. So when we say that during the next fifty years deforestation will destroy hundreds of thousands of species of plants and animals in these forests, how many new medicines, new food crops, natural insecticides, and oil-producing trees are we destroying? What will the effect be on our planet and on human life if we destroy so many kinds of animals and plants?

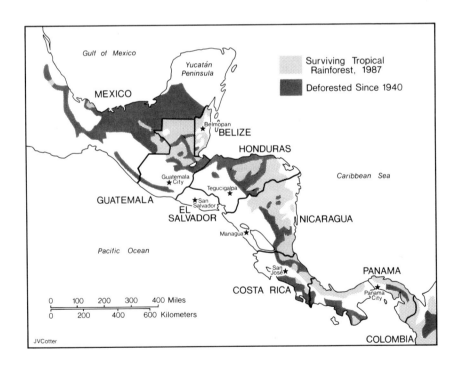

Left: *huge sections of Central America's tropical rainforests have fallen to axe and fire during the twentieth century. Deforestation in the region results from road construction, colonization by farm families, and clearing for export crops such as coffee and bananas. The majority of cleared land ends up as pasture for beef cattle, although production is usually cut short by erosion, weeds, and loss of nutrients. Above: smoke rises from burning rainforest in Chiapas, Mexico. Such deforestation claims huge areas of rainforest around the world each year.*

The answer to those questions is that we don't know. What we do know is that tropical rainforests and the species that live in them are being eradicated in many of the world's tropical countries. As these forests are cut down and burned, the plants that live in them go up in smoke. Some animals may manage to escape the burning forest and find temporary refuge in nearby uncut forest, but many times they die anyway because they must compete for food with the creatures that already live there.

At the rate rainforests are being cleared and burned, at least two dozen tropical countries that have rainforest today will have almost none by the time most of the readers of this book reach the age of sixty-five.

TROPICAL RAINFORESTS ARE
THREATENED WORLDWIDE

If you read several different books about tropical rainforests, you may see different figures cited about the amount of tropical rainforest destroyed around the world every year. These differences usually come about because different authors use different definitions for the term "tropical rainforest."

The two studies of tropical deforestation considered to be the most accurate say that between 24,000 and 30,000 square miles (62,000 to 80,000 square kilometers) of rainforest are cleared every year. What that means is that, around the world, humans are destroying between 28 and 35 acres (11 to 14 hectares) of tropical rainforest every minute—day and night. Joined together in one place, this would represent a block of rainforest the size of West Virginia destroyed every year![2]

Where tropical rainforests once took up about 6.5 million square miles (17 million square kilometers) of the earth's land area, today this territory has been reduced to only 3.5 million square miles (9.1 million square kilometers), an area about the size of the United States.[3]

SOME RAINFORESTS WILL SURVIVE

This is not to say that all the world's tropical rainforests are doomed to disappear. Tropical rainforests are being eradicated at different rates in different nations of the world. In fact, rainforests in some areas of the world are not in danger—at least, not yet.

In Africa, for example, the rainforests in the nations of Zaire, Gabon, and the Congo should survive for several more decades. And in South America, the rainforests of Guyana, Suriname, French Guiana, and of much of the western Brazilian Amazon should stand for at least another fifty years.

But predictions are not that bright for the majority of tropical countries. The continent of Africa as a whole is losing its rainforests at a very rapid rate. Combined, the nations of Africa have lost over 400,000 square miles (1,000,000 square kilometers) of rainforest during the past hundred years. That's an area almost the size of Texas and California combined.

Rainforest destruction is equally alarming in Southeast Asia. Large areas of the rainforests on the peninsula of Malaysia have been cleared or degraded. Burma, Thailand, and Laos are losing several thousand square miles of rainforest each year. Southeast Asia was also the scene of probably the fastest rate of rainforest destruction the world has ever seen. This occurred during the Vietnam War, when U.S. military forces eradicated tropical rainforests and mangrove forests to prevent the enemy from hiding there. About half the forest in South Vietnam was destroyed, and 2,000 square miles (5,000 square kilometers) of the tropical forest of North Vietnam were bombed or destroyed with chemicals.[4]

During 1982–83, wild fires swept through 14,000 square miles (36,000 square kilometers) of tropical rainforest of East Kalimantan, an Indonesian province on the island of Borneo. The amount of burned forest equaled an area the size of Taiwan. Severe drought and destructive

logging practices set the stage for the fires, which were set off by agricultural fires that escaped their bounds.[5]

Of all the continents, Latin America has the largest amount of tropical rainforest—about 2 million square miles (5 million square kilometers). This amounts to more than half the world's remaining tropical rainforest. But Latin America's current stand of rainforest represents only 60 percent of the tropical rainforest that once covered the region. Human activities have been wiping out 11,200 square miles (29,000 square kilometers) of Latin America's rainforests every year.

In one of the most ambitious development projects of all time, Brazil bulldozed the Transamazon Highway across the Amazon rainforest during the decade of the 1970s. Geographer Nigel Smith, who spent two and a half years in communities along the highway, says that political considerations were the chief reason for constructing the highway. The Brazilian government wanted to incorporate the Amazon rainforest into their national economy. They also hoped to transfer up to a million poor families into the region.

"The third major reason for the decision to build the Transamazon," Smith says, "was a desire to reach natural resources." Government planners saw the region as a vast source of tin, gold, and timber.

Not counting clearing by farm families and cattle ranchers, preparation for the highway destroyed a swath of forest 230 feet wide and 2,000 miles long (70 meters by 3,200 kilometers). Superimposed on a map of Europe, the high-

U.S. troops destroyed thousands of square miles of tropical rainforest in South and North Vietnam during the Vietnam War.

way would stretch from Moscow to Lisbon. But if we include deforestation by farmers and ranchers who followed the highway, the total amount of rainforest eradicated by the Transamazon Highway surpasses almost 72,000 square miles (190,000 square kilometers).

Today, the Transamazon is generally considered to be a giant project that failed. Most of the soils turned out to be unsuitable for long-term cultivation, and many families who followed the highway into the rainforest later returned to their original homes in other parts of Brazil. Although Brazil is taking out large amounts of timber and minerals such as gold and copper, they have traded these goods for the destruction of a large chunk of the Amazon rainforest. The highway has seriously disrupted the lives of many indigenous people who live in the Amazon Basin. In sum, says Smith, the Transamazon serves as an example of the pitfalls of schemes devised in offices far removed from where they are carried out.[6]

Farther north, in Mexico and Central America, almost two-thirds of the original tropical rainforest has been converted to other uses. When Europeans first reached the area four hundred years ago, Mexico and Central America were covered with 160,000 square miles (414,000 square kilometers) of tropical rainforest. But today, less than 50,000 square miles (130,000 square kilometers) remain. The rest have been destroyed by human activities.

Because of the speed at which the region's remaining rainforests are being cleared and burned, the final third of the tropical rainforests of Mexico and Central America may be eliminated within twenty-five years. The region may end up with nothing more than degraded remnants of tropical rainforests in national parks and forest reserves. The rainforests of Mexico and Central America join the rainforests of Indonesia, Malaysia, Thailand, Madagascar, West Africa, and several other regions as the most threatened rainforests in the world.

THE CAUSES OF
DEFORESTATION ARE COMPLEX

All of this information forces us to ask the question: If rainforests are so important, why are they being destroyed in the first place?

The best way to understand the complex web of reasons why tropical deforestation occurs is to look at one particular area in detail. The rainforest region that lies closest to the United States serves as a good example. This is the tropical rainforest of Central America. In this region of tropical America, the causes of tropical deforestaton can be broken down into three stages.

ROAD CONSTRUCTION

The first stage begins with the construction of roads. The outside world literally bulldozes its way into the rainforest by building new roads. These roads are built for a variety of reasons. Oil exploration and military control are two increasingly important reasons. Oil companies must build new roads through the forest to explore for oil and to extract it if they find it. Roads are part of military strategy in Central America because they allow governments to move troops into the region and to maintain control of borders with other countries.

But in most cases, rainforest roads are built in Central America to take out valuable timber. Logging companies bulldoze roads through the rainforest so they can use trucks to take out mahogany and tropical cedar. Removed from the rainforest, this timber ends up on international markets where it is used for office paneling, boats, and fine furniture.

To get these valuable trees, tropical loggers carry out what they call "creaming" or "high-grading" the forest. They remove only a few of the hundreds of trees that stand on each acre of forest. They are not doing this to conserve the forest. Instead, they are forced to work this way by the diversity of the tropical rainforest.

Because rainforests bear such an incredible range of plant life, you may find two hundred different tree species on a plot of 2.5 acres (1 hectare). But that also means that you'll find only a few individuals of the particular kind of tree you are searching for. Loggers have to bulldoze roads through large areas of forest to cut enough valuable trees to make a profit. When they find the trees, they use long cables or small tractors called "skidders" to pull out the few trees per acre that are commercially valuable.

You might predict—correctly—that this process destroys a lot of forest. Rainforest trees are tied to one another at the crown through an interconnected mass of vines and vegetation. When loggers pulls down one mahogany tree, surrounding trees come down with it. Also, as that tree falls, it will crush the trees it lands on. Studies indicate that felling a single commercially valuable tree can cause the destruction of an average of seventeen noncommercial trees. Considering this and the areas cleared for roads and loading areas, logging operations may end up destroying 30 percent of a rainforest where only a few trees per acre have been taken out and sold.[7]

COLONIZATION

The problem with logging, though, is not so much what the loggers take out as what they leave behind—namely, the roads they build to enter the forest in the first place. Roads introduce the second stage of rainforest destruction—colonization.

During this stage, landless farm families from other regions of the country, or even from other countries, file down these logging roads and create new jungle settlements. They clear what remains of the forest to raise subsistence crops like corn, beans, rice, and manioc, and cash crops like coffee, cacao, and sugarcane.

Colonists sometimes clear more land than they need for growing their crops because the most effective way to demonstrate to other people that they own the land is to "develop" it by clearing and burning its forest cover.

Some scientists and politicians have blamed colonizing farmers as the main reason for tropical deforestation in Central America. Others say this is like blaming soldiers for causing wars. Farm families do much of the work in clearing and burning tropical rainforest, but they're simply pawns in a bigger game. To understand the role of colonists in rainforest destruction, we have to ask why they are in the rainforest in the first place. And the answer to that question is that there's no land for them anywhere else. There are two reasons why this is true.

The first reason comes from the way farmland is distributed among different groups of people in Central America. Much of Central America's best agricultural lands are owned by a small group of families or companies in each of the countries. These families and companies dedicate these fertile lands to producing export crops—crops that can be sold overseas. The most common of these export crops are cotton, bananas, sugarcane, pineapples, cocoa, coffee, and cattle. Because the best soils are dedicated to export crops, the growing population of farm families is left with no farmland except small plots on hillsides and in forests. They are forced to use these areas because they have no access to better land.

In Guatemala, for example, 2 percent of the landowners control 72 percent of the farmland, most of which is dedicated to banana plantations, coffee farms, and cattle ranches. Meanwhile, 83 percent of the farm families either own no land or own too little to support themselves. In Costa Rica, 1 percent of the population owns 36 percent of the farm land, most of which is devoted to coffee, cotton, cattle, and sugarcane.

A Tzeltal Maya farmer dries jalapeño peppers over a fire in the rainforest of Chiapas, Mexico. The man will carry the dried peppers three hours down jungle trails to sell.

In sum, half the farm families in Central America either own no land or own too little to support a family. To buy food, they work as day laborers harvesting coffee, picking cotton, or cutting sugarcane. Or, if they are lucky, they eventually migrate to the rainforest to claim their own plot of land.

The second major reason that colonists migrate into the rainforest is population growth. Central America's population has tripled since 1945. At the rate the region's population is growing, the number of people in the region—now 25.1 million—will double in twenty-six years, reaching 60 million people by the year A.D. 2020. Every year, more people are trying to make a living farming the land. And as long as there is rainforest land left to colonize, landless families will continue to migrate into those forests and clear it to support themselves.

But, in the long run, the families hardly benefit from their role in forest destruction. Once they have cleared the rainforest vegetation for farms, their land quickly begins to deteriorate.

Burning the rainforest for agriculture or pastureland releases the nutrients of the burned vegetation in a flush of temporary fertility, but these nutrients are absorbed by the crops and harvested along with them. Most of the nutrients wash away with the rain, leaving the cleared area eroded and infertile. Unless the soils are carefully managed, weeds, insects, and declining soil fertility reduce crop yields after only a few years.

Faced with this problem, many families decide to move farther into the forest to clear more rainforest land. As their pioneer front moves through the forest, the landscape becomes a mosaic of eroded fields, pastureland, and scattered trees. Most of the area's wildlife disappears through habitat destruction and hunting by the farmers. The families remain trapped in a pattern of deforestation that prolongs their poverty.

THE SPECIAL CASE OF CATTLE

Although colonization of tropical rainforests in Central America wipes out much of the rainforest vegetation, this second stage of deforestation is almost always followed by a third. This stage focuses on the expansion of export crops into the rainforest, and this is basically the driving force behind deforestation.

During this stage, the land that colonizing farm families have cleared is absorbed by a second wave of settlers who follow behind the farmers buying up their small farms. They combine these farms into large plantations to produce export crops. These crops include coffee, cacao, citrus fruits, and African oil palm, but the most dominant and most destructive of these export products is beef cattle.

Cattle ranchers obtain the land of colonist families in several different ways. The farm families may willingly sell the land they've cleared when weeds, insects, and declining fertility overpower their farming methods. Because they have no money for fertilizer and because no farming specialists are on the scene to teach them how to raise crops year after year on the same soils, they simply sell their land to the cattle ranchers and move on to clear more forest.

In other cases, colonization and cattle production are combined. In the Darién rainforest of southern Panama, colonists settle on national forest land, clear it, burn it, and then sell it for thirty-two dollars an acre to weekend cattle ranchers from Panama City. These new urban landowners are not interested in producing cattle as much as they're interested in holding on to the land as an investment.

No matter how the land is originally cleared, the end result is the same. After five to ten years of mediocre beef yields, erosion, weeds, and loss of fertility prompt the cattle ranchers to search for new pasturelands. Like the farmers before them, the cattle ranchers move farther into the forest and clear more land, and repeat the cycle until the rainforest is gone.

Cattle graze on cleared rainforest land
in Chiapas, Mexico. Clearing forest for
pasture is one of the most common reasons
for rainforest destruction in Latin America.

The tragedy of converting farmland and rainforest to cattle pasture is apparent on several levels. First is the poor yield that cattle ranching produces on cleared rainforest land. The average number of cattle on cleared Central American rainforest lands is one head for every 4 acres (2 hectares) of land. The average yield is 9 pounds (4 kilograms) of beef per acre per year. As a comparison, on the same amount of land, a traditional Lacandon Maya farmer can produce *5,000 pounds* (2,300 kilograms) of shelled corn per acre and another 4,000 pounds (1,800 kilograms) of root crops and tree crops. Yet cattle production is replacing the Lacandon Maya farming system and others like it.

Transforming forest into cattle pasture also fails to aid the colonists who live in rainforest cattle areas. In the first place, raising cattle requires less labor than other production systems, so few jobs are created. But more important is the fact that the beef produced on this land is exported out of the area, either to consumers in the Central American cities or to other countries.

In fact, beef importing companies in the United States buy between 20 percent and 33 percent of all the beef produced in Central America, part of which is raised on cleared rainforest land. Most of this meat goes into luncheon meats, frankfurters, chili, beef stew, soups, sausages, TV dinners, baby foods, and pet foods. Several groups in the United States are working to prevent the continuing import of rainforest-produced beef into the country on the grounds that it is a destructive, inefficient industry.

THE LEGACY OF DEFORESTATION

Development projects such as hydroelectric dams also eradicate large areas of tropical rainforest. For example, during the mid-1970s, the construction of the Bayano hydroelectric project in Panama destroyed 140 square miles

(360 square kilometers) of agricultural land and tropical rainforest to create a reservoir that is already silting in as a result of deforestation. The Tucuruí Dam in the Amazon rainforest will flood more than 760 square miles (2,000 square kilometers) of forest. It is the fourth largest dam in the world.[8]

Taken together, this combination of road construction, logging, colonization, cattle ranching, and development projects is now replacing Central America's tropical rainforests at the rate of more than 1,600 square miles (4,100 square kilometers) per year. Many of the region's cloud forests, because of their rugged terrain and humid climate, had until recently remained more or less intact. But these forests, too, are being threatened by the expansion of coffee growing, cattle ranching, and colonists' farming.

Combined with the ongoing degradation of coniferous forests and dry tropical forests, this massive conversion of tropical rainforests is the most dramatic environmental change ever experienced in Central America's history.

6
Protecting
Tropical
Rainforests

*This we know—the earth does not belong to man,
man belongs to the earth. All things are connected
like the blood which unites one family. Man did
not weave the web of life; he is merely a strand
in it. Whatever he does to the web,
he does to himself.*

Chief Sealth of the
Duwamish Tribe
of Washington State[1]

Froilan Payaguaje, a Siona Indian, lives in a palm-roofed house built on stilts in the tropical rainforest of eastern Ecuador. Past his house rushes the dark Tarapuy River, stained tea color by natural chemicals in the leaves of the forest vegetation. Downstream, the river flows into three others before merging into the largest river in the world, the Amazon.

For centuries, Payaguaje's Siona ancestors lived in this rainforest, enjoying a bounty of fish and turtles, hunting

Siona Indian park guard Froilan Payaguaje
patrols the Cuyabeno Wildlife Reserve in
the Amazon rainforest of eastern Ecuador.
This reserve protects 1,000 square miles
(2,600 square kilometers) of Ecuador's tropical
rainforest as well as the Siona's territory.

monkeys and agoutis, and harvesting manioc and corn from small garden clearings. Life was much the same for hundreds of years.

But Froilan Payaguaje's life is different. When the sun rises each morning, he's more likely to head for his canoe than to go hunting or work in his garden plot. Payaguaje is the head park guard in the Cuyabeno Wildlife Production Reserve, a new conservation area operated by Ecuador's national parks department. The Cuyabeno Reserve protects 1,000 square miles (2,600 square kilometers) of Amazon rainforest and the traditional territory of the Siona Indians. Payaguaje spends his days—and many of his evenings— seeing to it that the reserve protects the plants, wildlife, and people who live within it.

In a 30-foot (9-meter) canoe with an outboard motor attached to the back, Payaguaje travels the rivers of the Cuyabeno Reserve. He talks with Siona relatives at their houses along the river. He visits families of colonists who have migrated into the rainforest, settling along the re-serve's borders. And he guides visiting tourists through the park, pointing out harpy eagles, anacondas, manatees, and river dolphins and making sure that everyone knows the rules.

From time to time, Payaguaje visits the headquarters and wells of the Ecuadorian corporation that pumps oil (Ecuador's most valuable export) from beneath the rain-forest floor. He monitors the company's actions to avoid oil spills and to protect the reserve's fragile ecosystems.

Froilan Payaguaje is part of a team of Ecuadorians who are exploring ways the Cuyabeno Reserve can improve the lives of the people who live within it or on its borders. The parks department hires Siona Indians and farmers from the surrounding area as park guards. Sionas serve as guides for the thousands of tourists who visit Cuyabeno every year.

On the reserve's borders, Payaguaje is working with biologists from Ecuador's national parks department and with local colonists to increase the number of wild animals such as capybaras, caimans, and iguanas. When wildlife populations reach a suitable level, they will begin to harvest the animals for meat. In such a fashion, Payaguaje and the national parks department are finding ways to cooperate with the Indian inhabitants of the Cuyabeno Reserve, and with the thousands of colonists who have settled along its borders.

Froilan Payaguaje's work in the Cuyabeno Reserve is an example of a new wave of action in tropical rainforest protection. The rapid increase in the number of people living in the world's tropical forests have prompted new ways of looking at tropical forest conservation. *Conservationists* (people who work for the protection and wise use of natural resources) now say that the need to preserve our planet's tropical rainforests must be balanced with the needs of human communities. If families are forced to invade national parks to stay alive, they say, we can be certain that they will do so.

Today, conservationists report that national parks and wildlife reserves must go beyond the traditional goals of protecting species and preserving wildlife habitat. Protected areas must also serve human beings if we expect these areas to survive.

This new blend of conservation and human concerns is considered so important that the last meeting of the World Congress on National Parks (a meeting held once every ten years) had as its theme this issue of balancing parks and people. One delegate to the congress stated the point clearly: "The people, the forest, and the wildlife either thrive together in a balanced environment, or stagnate together in a wretched one."[2]

THE FUTURE OF
TROPICAL RAINFORESTS

Conservationists say that the fate of our planet's rainforests is being decided during the decades that we are now living. Whether or not these unique environments survive to benefit future generations, they say, depends on actions taken during the next fifty years.

Many scientists feel that conserving these forests is one of the most important issues of the twentieth century. They are working to protect the forests that remain, and they are making good progress. Despite the rapid destruction of our planet's tropical rainforests, solutions and alternatives do exist. Deforestation can be halted in many tropical nations, and rainforests can be used wisely for the benefit of human beings—without destroying the forests.[3]

One of the most important activities taking place in rainforest conservation is the creation and protection of tropical rainforest parks and reserves like the Cuyabeno Wildlife Production Reserve. Countries throughout the tropics can be proud of the impressive array of national parks, forest reserves, and other protected rainforest areas that already exist. National parks and reserves protect more than 60,000 square miles (160,000 square kilometers) of tropical rainforest around the world.[4]

Some of these areas are undisturbed forest wilderness with tapirs, pacas, reptiles, monkeys, and a range of rainforest species. Others are small pockets of rainforest surrounded by human populations. But all these protection areas conserve important species of the rainforest ecosystem.

BIOSPHERE RESERVES

Conservationists continue to try new ideas for the growing system of protected rainforest areas. One idea now spreading rapidly is the *biosphere reserve*, a kind of conservation area first promoted by the United Nations Educational, Scientific and Cultural Organization (UNESCO). In line with conservationists' new way of looking at wild lands and human populations, biosphere reserves combine forest preservation with the needs of nearby human communities.

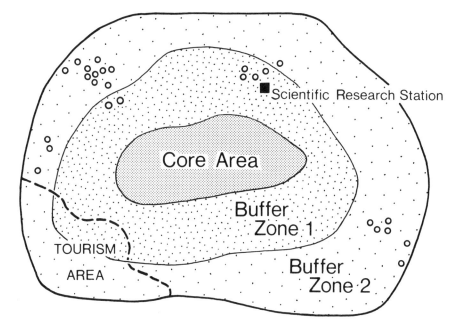

Scientific Research Station

Core Area

Buffer Zone 1

TOURISM AREA

Buffer Zone 2

○ Human Settlement

Biosphere reserves, a concept originated by United Nations scientists, offer great hope for the protection of tropical rainforests. Biosphere reserves combine the production of food and other products that benefit human beings with the conservation of the reserve's plant and animal species. Both people and rainforests prosper in this new type of conservation area.

Biosphere reserves have various zones, and each zone has different rules. One zone is always an unviolated core of natural vegetation that is permanently protected. This core area is surrounded by concentric rings of land used by the reserve's human residents. Conservationists call these outer rings *buffer zones*. Local people may gather medicinal plants or harvest wild foods from the first buffer zone. Scientists and tourists enter to take photographs and collect specimens. In the next concentric ring out, local families farm and collect wood. And in the outer rings appear houses, hotels, and roads.

Tribal people are encouraged to use the outer rings of the reserve much as they have used the forest for centuries. Immigrant farm families who live on the edges of reserves are included in planning efforts so that they have an interest in the reserve's success. These families serve as the guardians of the buffer zone and of the protected inner core. Almost 250 biosphere reserves now exist in 65 countries, though only one-fourth of these protect tropical rainforest.[5]

The crucial point about biosphere reserves—and more and more about all types of rainforest parks and reserves— is that local people are included in their planning and development.

THE SAN BLAS KUNA

One of the best examples of this new approach to rainforest conservation is the Kuna Indian nature reserve in Panama. The Kuna are a tribe of thirty thousand Native Americans who live in villages on islands along the coast of Panama and at the mouths of several rivers that flow through their territory into the Caribbean Sea. The Kuna's tribal territory, called the Comarca de San Blas, covers more than 1,240 square miles (3,210 square kilometers) of tropical rainforest. Kuna families plant corn, manioc, yams, and bananas in rainforest clearings on the mainland. They also fish and grow coconuts on the islands that line Panama's Caribbean coast. Almost all the Kuna's land is still covered with tropical rainforest.

*These Kuna Indians live in the Kuna
Indian nature preserve in Panama.*

The Kuna say that their rainforest is the home of po-
tentially evil spirits that will rise up in anger and attack
their communities if their forest home is disturbed. To protect themselves from these spirits, the Kuna protect the
rainforest itself. They harvest food and materials from the
forest, but they take only what they need. They view the
rainforest as their combination drugstore and refrigerator.
They gather medicinal plants to combat illnesses, and they

eat plants and animals that they find in the forest. But the rest they conserve.

The Kuna became concerned about the future of their rainforest environment when they saw the forest in much of the rest of Panama being cleared and burned for agriculture and cattle ranching. To prevent the deforestation of their own land, in 1983 they declared a large part of their tribal territory a nature reserve. They made this decision on their own, then hired scientists and park planners to help them bring their vision to reality. Today, Kuna park managers and Kuna guards watch over the first rainforest park in the world that was created by a tribal group.

As part of this park, the Kuna created a botanical garden with rainforest trees labeled with their Kuna, Spanish, and scientific names. They have programs of scientific tourism that allow photographers and scientists to enter and study the area. Scientists travel to the Kuna nature reserve to carry out research. They pay the Kuna to serve as guides in the rainforest, and they pay for the privilege of using Kuna land as their natural laboratory.

For the Kuna, scientific tourism means new jobs and more income for their communities. At the same time, the reserve means that the Kuna can preserve their tribal identity and their rainforest home.[6]

Many researchers believe that far more rainforest land must be conserved throughout the tropics if we expect the diversity of these forests to survive. In his book *The Sinking Ark*, conservation writer Norman Myers writes that 10 to 20 percent of the remaining tropical rainforest should be protected.

But so far, only 3 percent of the rainforest of Africa has come under protection. Only 2 percent is protected in Southeast Asia, and only 1 percent of South America's tropical rainforest is protected in national parks or reserves. Myers says that many more rainforest parks and reserves must be created if we hope to realize the goal of protecting samples of all the world's rainforest habitats.[7]

ATTACKING ROOT PROBLEMS

National parks and reserves are a crucial part of the conservation of the world's tropical rainforests, but their creation is only one of many steps being taken. Equally important in conservationists' views is action to address the economic and social factors that lead to deforestation in the first place.

For example, some researchers are concentrating on improving logging techniques so that tropical countries can harvest valuable timber from their rainforests without destroying the forest that remains. These scientists say that forests can be protected during logging if companies take extreme care when they decide where roads are to be built. They can also leave strips of protection forest next to rivers and lakes.

Foresters are also learning how to fell trees in a predetermined direction so that falling trees damage less of the surrounding rainforest. Other scientists are working to plant man-made forests in tropical nations, so that people will not be forced to cut down rainforests to get wood.[8]

Still other researchers are working with international development banks to identify projects such as hydroelectric dams or colonization programs that may destroy rainforests. They suggest alternative sites and projects that will protect tropical forests while promoting human welfare.

PLANTING FORESTS WITH FOOD

Another important priority is research on new ways of farming in the rainforest. Researchers in several nations of Africa, Asia, and Latin America are working to find farming systems that can produce crops without destroying the rainforest. These farming systems are aimed at improving crop yields and farmers' incomes, but conserving the rainforest at the same time.

Instead of clearing more land for farming every year, farmers can learn how to harvest the same plots of land year after year. They do this by managing the land more carefully—by controlling water and by keeping the soil covered with trees that are crops themselves—timber trees, fuelwood trees, and fruit trees.

One of the best examples of these farming systems is *agroforestry*. Agroforestry means that farmers plant trees with their crops instead of clearing trees in order to plant crops. Scientists at the Center for Tropical Agriculture Research and Teaching (CATIE) in Costa Rica are working with farmers to produce food crops, firewood trees, lumber trees, and cash crops such as coffee and cacao on the same farmland. Because agroforestry combines farming with the advantages of a standing forest, it is an effective farming technique for tropical regions.

In an agroforestry system, for example, a farmer may plant food crops as he normally would in jungle agriculture, but he also plants tree crops such as rubber, cacao, coffee, citrus, or nuts on the same plot at the same time. By the time the farmer is ready to harvest his food crops, the trees have grown enough to protect the soil and prevent soil erosion and loss of nutrients. Later, the area beneath the tree crops may be planted in crops that can tolerate shade or it may be dedicated entirely to tree production. Years later, when the farmer finally cuts down the trees, he replants the area in food crops and begins the cycle anew.

Coffee, bananas, fuelwood trees, and lumber trees grow at different levels in this agroforestry plot in Costa Rica. Agroforestry is a good system in tropical rainforests because farmers plant trees along with their food and cash crops.

Agroforestry systems allow farmers to utilize each forest plot continually, rather than for only two or three years, then letting the plots regrow and regenerate—a period called fallowing the land.

TROPICAL CHINAMPAS

Another promising farming system is actually an ancient system rediscovered. This is the tropical *chinampa* being developed in Mexico. You may have heard of the floating gardens of Xochimilco, near Mexico City. But the gardens don't really float. They're chinampas—garden plots made by mounding soil on strips of land in areas where water is available year-round. Chinampas are usually constructed in swampy areas or near a river or lake. Researchers call them one of the most productive methods of farming ever devised. When well cared for, chinampas can produce several crops per year and remain fertile for centuries.

A farmer creates a chinampa system by digging trenches, or canals, on at least three sides of his garden plots. He adds the soil he takes out of the canals to the garden plot. As he digs deeper, water seeps into the ditches and turns each of the garden plots into an island. He then plants his crops in the island plots.

The soil on chinampas stays fertile because the farmer periodically dredges the mud from the canals and adds it to the cultivation plots as organic fertilizer. Aquatic vegetation that grows in the canals serves as "green manure."

A wealth of food crops grow in this tropical chinampa in Tabasco, Mexico. Chinampas —garden plots surrounded by irrigation-drainage canals— produce crops year round.

(120)

The water canals allow the farmer to control his crops' water supply. He uses the canals to irrigate plants during the dry season and to drain off excess water during the rainy season. Fish that colonize the canals provide his family with high-quality protein.

Experiments conducted on chinampas in tropical rain-forest areas in Mexico show that tropical chinampas maintain year-round production of food and cash crops. They produce constant and abundant harvests in areas that people thought were too wet for farming. Experimental chinampas have produced food and cash crops for a family of ten people on 2.5 acres (1 hectare) of land. And they do this year after year without depleting the soil and without requiring the farmer to clear new forest land.

Another benefit of the chinampa system comes from the fact that the farmer plants trees along the canals to hold the soil in place. Depending on the tree species he selects, he can produce additional food, fiber, and fuelwood. Planting trees also creates wind barriers and habitat for insect-eating birds.

The chinampa system does not require machinery, insecticides, or artificial fertilizers, although the farmer can use any of these additions if he chooses. The system is also compatible with cattle production, because crop residues and weeds from the chinampas can be used as fodder for cattle. In return, the cattle provide meat and milk, and their wastes are added to the cultivation plots as organic fertilizer.[9]

If scientists and local farmers succeed at creating large areas of tropical chinampas in Mexico and other tropical countries, they will be recreating a system once used by the Aztecs of Mexico and by the ancient Maya. The Aztec empire emerged during the fourteenth and fifteenth centuries in the lake bed now covered by Mexico City. The Aztecs used chinampas to feed the entire city that was their headquarters.

Farther south in Latin America, from A.D. 250 to A.D. 900, the Maya created between 600 and 1,000 square miles (1,600 to 2,600 square kilometers) of chinampas in the tropical rainforest region of Mexico, Guatemala, and Belize. This system grew the food for a civilization that flourished in the rainforest for ten centuries.[10]

Today, as farmers create new tropical chinampas in the same region of Latin America, they are rediscovering an ancient farming system that once supported millions of people in harmony with the tropical rainforest.

The main benefit of farming systems like agroforestry and tropical chinampas is that they allow families to harvest the same plots of land year after year without destroying forests. Because the farmers remain on the same plots of land, they do not have to clear more forest every year. The farmers also prosper because they can produce more crops to eat and sell. For this reason, part of the key to rainforest conservation lies outside the rainforest itself—in the farming techniques of rural families.[11]

Other activities are also important in determining the future of tropical rainforests. Some researchers say that distributing land more equally in tropical countries would go far in defusing the push of landless farm families into tropical rainforests. But these researchers also point out that, no matter how fairly land is distributed, if we expect tropical forests to survive, rapid population growth must be slowed.[12]

7
Epilogue: What Can I Do?

If you feel concerned enough about tropical rainforests to want to do something to insure that they survive, learn everything you can about them and teach others about their importance to life on earth. The more you know about tropical rainforests, the more effectively you can act to conserve them. Reading other books about rainforests and watching documentaries on rainforest wildlife are effective ways to learn more.

The responsibility for conserving the world's tropical rainforests does not lie just in the countries where these forests exist. Citizens in the developed nations have an equal responsibility. Some of the products that cause rainforest destruction end up in our restaurants and in our kitchens. Part of conserving tropical rainforests is finding out how our consumer habits affect these forests and changing those habits, if necessary.

Learning about rainforests may make you want to visit one. Set yourself the goal of someday visiting a national park or reserve someplace in the tropical world. There, you'll be able to touch and smell the reality of the tropical rainforest in an unforgettable on-the-ground experience.

In the meantime, there are important things you can do to help conserve tropical rainforests, no matter where you live. Citizens can work for the wise use and conservation of tropical rainforests by organizing environmental education projects that explain the value of tropical rainforests and teach others about them. If your school has a science fair, consider doing a project on rainforest ecology or rainforest conservation. Find out if your school has educational materials—guidebooks and posters—about tropical rainforests and their products.

Also, consider joining one of the wide range of environmental groups and citizen organizations working to counter unnecessary tropical rainforest destruction. You'll find a list of some of them at the end of this chapter.

If there's a zoo in your hometown, visit it and support it. Ask what you can do to help protect endangered species. If you shop for a pet, don't buy an animal that was taken from a tropical rainforest. Monkeys, parrots, and other tropical birds are sometimes brought into the country illegally and sold as pets. When you buy a pet, make sure that it was raised in captivity, not taken from the wild. As the store manager for proof of the animal's origin.

Finally, ask your school's biology teacher about careers related to tropical rainforests. You may want to learn more about careers as a zoologist, anthropologist, ethnobotanist, geographer, photographer, or writer. All these careers can promote the survival of tropical rainforests and other vital ecosystems.

Two excellent books about the earth's ecosystems and their protection are *Gaia: An Atlas of Planet Management*, edited by Norman Myers, and Lee Durrell's *State of the Ark: An Atlas of Conservation in Action*.

Individuals *can* make a difference. Working with conservation organizations and with citizens in the tropical world, people can create positive change and help alter destructive patterns that are threatening important natural resources.

Short of nuclear war, the most crucial problems the planet will face during your lifetime will be ecological problems like food production, population growth, and deforestation. These problems are complex, but there are none that are more important. Acting as individuals and in groups, people can solve these problems and help create a world where human beings and other species can live in harmony and prosper.

ORGANIZATIONS WORKING TO CONSERVE TROPICAL RAINFORESTS

Conservation International
1015 18th Street, N.W., Suite 1000
Washington, D.C. 20036

Environmental Defense Fund
1616 P Street, N.W.
Washington, D.C. 20036

International Union for the
Conservation of Nature and
Natural Resources (IUCN)
Av. du Mont Blanc
1196 Gland
Switzerland

National Audubon Society
International Wildlife Program
801 Pennsylvania Avenue, S.E.
Washington, D.C. 20003

National Wildlife Federation
International Program
1412 16th Street, N.W.
Washington, D.C. 20036

National Zoological Park
Smithsonian Institution
Washington, D.C. 20008

The Nature Conservancy
International Program
1785 Massachusetts Avenue, N.W.
Washington, D.C. 20036

Rainforest Action Network
466 Green Street., Suite 300
San Francisco, California 94133

TRAFFIC (U.S.A.)
1250 24th Street, N.W.
Washington, D.C. 20037

Tropical Ecosystem Research and Rescue
P.O. Box 18391
Washington, D.C. 20036

Wildlife Conservation International
New York Zoological Society
Bronx, New York, 10460

World Wide Fund for Nature
Av. du Mont Blanc
1196 Gland
Switzerland

World Wildlife Fund/
The Conservation Foundation
1250 24th Street, N.W.
Washington, D.C. 20037

Notes

Introduction

1. Norman Myers, ed. *Gaia: An Atlas of Planet Management* (Garden City, N.Y.: Anchor Press/Doubleday, 1984), p. 30.
2. Norman Myers, *The Sinking Ark: A New Look at the Problem of Disappearing Species* (New York: Pergamon Press, 1979), pp. 113–129.
3. World Resources Institute, *Tropical Forests: A Call for Action* (Washington, D.C.: World Resources Institute, 1985), p. *v.*

Chapter 1: What Are Tropical Rainforests?

1. Donald Perry, *Life Above the Jungle Floor: A Biologist Explores a Strange and Hidden Treetop World* (New York: Simon and Schuster, 1986), p. 14.
2. Catherine Caufield, *In the Rainforest: Report from a Strange, Beautiful, Imperiled World* (New York: Alfred A. Knopf, 1985), p. 62.

3. Peter T. White, "Tropical Rain Forests: Nature's Dwindling Treasures," *National Geographic* vol. 163, no. 1 (1983): pp. 2–48.
4. Marston Bates, *Where Winter Never Comes: A Study of Man and Nature in the Tropics* (New York: Charles Scribner's Sons, 1963).
5. Norman Myers, *Conversion of Tropical Moist Forests* (Washington, D.C.: National Academy of Sciences, 1980).

Chapter 2: Wonders of the Tropical Rainforest

1. Perry, p. 14.
2. Edward S. Ayensu, ed., *Jungles* (New York: Crown, 1980), p. 64.
3. Communication with Dr. Merlin D. Tuttle, science director of Bat Conservation International.
4. Adrian Forsyth and Ken Miyata, *Tropical Nature: Life and Death in the Rain Forests of Central and South America* (New York: Charles Scribner's Sons, 1984), p. 104.
5. Ayensu, pp. 144–147.
6. Caufield, p. 64.

Chapter 3: The Importance of Tropical Rainforests

1. Garrison Wilkes, "The World's Crop Plant Germ Plasm—an Endangered Resource," *The Bulletin of the Atomic Scientists*, vol. 33, no. 2 (1977): p. 16.
2. Edgar Anderson, *Plants, Man and Life* (Berkeley, California: University of California Press, 1952), Chapter 10; Roger Revelle, "Flying Beans, Botanical Whales, Jack's Beanstalk, and Other Marvels," *The National Research Council in 1978* (Washington, D.C.: National Academy of Sciences, 1978).

3. Ayensu, p. 185.
4. James H. Cock, "Cassava Research," *Field Crops Research*, vol. 2 (Amsterdam: Elsevier Scientific, 1979), pp. 185–191.
5. Myers, *The Sinking Ark*, p. 122.
6. Noel Vietmeyer, Speech on "Human Dependence on Biological Diversity," National Forum on Biodiversity, National Academy of Sciences/Smithsonian Institution, Washington, D.C. (September 1986).
7. Myers, *The Sinking Ark*, p. 147.
8. Office of Technology Assessment, *Technologies to Sustain Tropical Forest Resources* (Washington, D.C.: Office of Technology Assessment, Congress of the United States, 1984), p. 51.
9. Nicholas Wade, "Waiting for the Oil Bug," *Science*, vol. 206 (1979): p. 1053.
10. Thomas H. Maugh, II, "Unlike Money, Diesel Fuel Grows on Trees," *Science*, vol. 206, no. 4417 (1979): p. 436.
11. Caufield, p. 230.
12. Caufield, p. 71.
13. Robert A. Goodland and H. W. Irwin, *Amazon Jungle: Green Hell to Red Desert?* (New York: Elsevier Scientific, 1975).
14. Frank Wadsworth, "Deforestation—Death to the Panama Canal," *Proceedings of the U.S. Strategy Conference on Tropical Deforestation.* (Washington, D.C.: U.S. Department of State, U.S. Agency for International Development), p. 23.
15. Myers, *Gaia*, pp. 116–117.
16. Peter Steinhart, "Trouble in the Tropics," *National Wildlife*, vol. 22, no. 1 (1984): p. 16.

Chapter 4: People of the Tropical Rainforest

1. Myers, *The Sinking Ark*, p. 122.

2. Mark J. Plotkin, *Ethnobotany and Conservation of the Tropical Forest with Special Reference to the Indians of Southern Suriname* (Ph.D. Dissertation, Tufts University, 1986), p. 335.
3. Virginia Morell, "Jungle Rx," *International Wildlife*, vol. 14, no. 5 (1984): pp. 18–24.
4. Richard Evans Schultes, "The Amazonia as a Source of New Economic Plants," *Economic Botany*, vol. 33, no. 3 (1980): p. 264.
5. Bayard Webster, "Tropical Forests Prove Cornucopia to Humans There," *New York Times*, Sunday, November 4, 1984.
6. Stephen Elliott and Joseph Brimacombe. "Searching for Cures in the Rainforest," *World Wildlife Fund News*, no. 3 (Morges, Switzerland, 1986).
7. Mark J. Plotkin, *Conservation and Ethnobotany in Tropical South America* (Washington, D.C.: World Wildlife Fund–U.S., 1984), p. 16.
8. Carl Djerassi, "The Making of the Pill," *Science 84*, vol. 5, no. 9 (1984): pp. 127–129.
9. Catherine Caufield, "Pioneers of the Outer Islands," *Natural History*, vol. 93, no. 3 (1984): p. 32.

Chapter 5: Tropical Rainforests in Danger

1. Paul Ehrlich and Anne Ehrlich, *Extinction: The Causes and Consequences of the Disappearance of Species* (New York: Random House, 1981). The controversy about the number of species being eradicated is examined in Edward C. Wolf, *On the Brink of Extinction: Conserving the Diversity of Life*, Worldwatch Paper No. 78 (Washington, D.C.: Worldwatch Institute, 1987), p. 11.
2. Norman Myers, *Conversion of Tropical Moist Forests*; Jean-Paul Lanly, *Tropical Forest Resources*, FAO Forestry Paper No. 30 (Rome: Food and Agriculture Or-

ganization of the United Nations, 1982); J. M. Melillo, C. A. Palm, R. A. Houghton, G. M. Woodwell, and Norman Myers, "Comparison of Two Recent Estimates of Disturbance in Tropical Forests," *Environmental Conservation*, vol. 12, no. 1 (1985): pp. 37–40.

3. Norman Myers, *The Primary Source: Tropical Forests and Our Future*, (New York: W. W. Norton, 1984), Chapter 9.
4. William A. Buckingham, *Operation Ranch Hand: The Air Force and Herbicides in Southeast Asia 1961–1971* (Washington, D.C.: U.S. Government Printing Office, 1982); Lee Durrell, *State of the Ark: An Atlas of Conservation in Action* (New York: Doubleday, 1986), p. 175.
5. Cynthia Mackie, "The Lessons Behind East Kalimantan's Forest Fires," *Borneo Research Bulletin*, vol. 16, no. 2 (1984): pp. 63–74.
6. Nigel J. H. Smith, *Rainforest Corridors: The Transamazon Colonization Scheme* (Berkeley and Los Angeles: University of California Press, 1982), p. 186.
7. Myers, *The Primary Source*, p. 106.
8. Catherine Caufield, "Dam the Amazon, Full Steam Ahead," *Natural History* (July 1983): pp. 60–67.

Chapter 6: Protecting Tropical Rainforests

1. Speech by Chief Sealth, reprinted in *Greenpeace Chronicles* (September 1979). Chief Sealth's name was later corrupted to Seattle, the name of the city built in the middle of the Duwamish tribe's land.
2. Jeffrey A. McNeeley and Kenton R. Miller, *National Parks, Conservation, and Development: The Role of Protected Areas in Sustaining Society* (Washington, D.C.: Smithsonian Institution Press, 1984), p. 183.
3. Myers, *The Primary Source*, Chapters 16–19.
4. Myers, *The Sinking Ark*, p. 222.

5. Michel Batisse, "The Biosphere Reserve: A Tool for Environmental Conservation and Management," *Environmental Conservation*, vol. 9, no. 2 (1982): pp. 101–111; Michel Batisse, "Action Plan for Biosphere Reserves" (Environmental Conservation, vol. 12, no. 1 (1985): pp. 17–27.

6. Patrick Breslin and Mac Chapin, "Land-Saving, Kuna Style." *Audubon*, vol. 86, no. 4 (1984): pp. 40–43.

7. Myers, *The Sinking Ark*, p. 222.

8. Myers, *The Primary Source*, pp. 106–108; Durrell, p. 53.

9. Michael D. Coe, "The Chinampas of Mexico," *Scientific American*, vol. 211, no. 1 (1964): pp. 90–98.

10. Adams, Richard E. W., "Ancient Maya Canals: Grids and Lattices in the Maya Jungle," *Archaeology*, vol. 35, no. 6 (1982): pp. 28–35.

11. Robert Goodland, "Environmental Ranking of Amazonian Development Projects in Brazil," *Environmental Conservation*, vol. 7, no. 1 (1980): pp. 9–26.

12. Erik Eckholm, *The Dispossessed of the Earth: Land Reform and Sustainable Development*, Worldwatch Paper No. 30. (Washington, D.C.: Worldwatch Institute, 1979), p. 41.

Glossary

agroforestry: farming systems in which farmers plant trees *with* crops, instead of removing trees in order to plant crops.

alkaloid: a complex organic compound containing nitrogen, found chiefly in plants and of interest because of their physiological effects. Morphine, strychnine, and nicotine are alkaloids.

biosphere reserve: a type of conservation area recognized by the United Nations Educational, Scientific and Cultural Organization (UNESCO). In these reserves, a protected inner core is surrounded by other zones that allow human use. Biosphere reserves frequently include tribal peoples and protect their land and traditions.

buffer zones: areas that border on a national park or biosphere reserve but are designed for use by humans as farming areas or for harvesting wildlife or plants.

buttresses: fanlike roots that support some rainforest trees above the thin forest soil.

canopy: the broad, interconnecting crowns of rainforest

(135)

trees, which form an almost continuous ceiling of green.

chinampas: farming systems in which the farmer mounds soil on top of garden plots in areas where water is available year-round.

conservationists: people who work for the protection and wise use of natural resources such as rainforests and wildlife.

deforestation: the destruction of forests, usually by cutting and burning.

ecosystem: a system formed by the interaction of a community or plants and animals with their environment.

emergents: the tallest trees of the rainforest, those that poke their heads above the canopy.

epiphytes: plants that grow on another plant for support and anchorage, rather than for nutrients. Orchids are the most common epiphytes in tropical rainforests.

ethnobotanists: scientists who combine the disciplines of botany and anthropology to study plant use by tribal peoples.

forest floor: the bottom layer of the tropical rainforest.

germ plasm: the protoplasm containing the units of heredity: the genes and chromosomes.

habitat: the type of natural environment in which a plant or animal lives. A habitat is determined mainly by vegetation.

lianas: woody vines, or climbers, of the tropical rainforest.

mimicry: similarity in appearance or behavior between two animals that gives protection against predators. In Batesian mimicry, a harmless creature imitates a dangerous or bad-tasting one to gain protection.

nutrients: the chemical food substances that organisms consume as food.

photosynthesis: the conversion by green plants of the sun's energy into carbohydrates from carbon dioxide and water.

shaman: a tribal medicine man who uses plants and animals to cure diseases among his people.

species: a group of animals similar in structure that are able to breed and produce viable young among themselves.

tropical zone: the region of the earth between the Tropic of Cancer and the Tropic of Capricorn, two imaginary lines equidistant from the earth's poles.

understory: the middle layer of the rainforest, between the canopy and forest floor.

Bibliography

Ayensu, Edward S., ed. *Jungles*. New York: Crown, 1980.
One of the most colorful and comprehensive of the general books on tropical rainforests, edited by a biologist from the Smithsonian Institution in Washington, D.C.

Bates, Marston. *Where Winter Never Comes: A Study of Man and Nature in the Tropics*. New York: Charles Scribner's Sons, 1963.
Personal narrative about tropical rainforests by the late Marston Bates, one of the United States' best-known biologists.

Caufield, Catherine. *In the Rainforest: Report from a Strange, Beautiful, Imperiled World*. New York: Alfred A. Knopf, 1985.
Based on interviews and field research around the world, this is one of the finest descriptions of the complexity of the ecology, development, and conservation of the world's tropical rainforests.

Durrell, Lee. *State of the Ark: An Atlas of Conservation in Action*. New York: Doubleday, 1986.

Ehrlich, Paul and Anne Ehrlich. *Extinction: The Causes and Consequences of the Disappearance of Species.* New York: Random House, 1981.

Forsyth, Adrian and Ken Miyata. *Tropical Nature: Life and Death in the Rain Forests of Central and South America.* New York: Charles Scribner's Sons, 1984.
Well-written and fascinating personal account of research in Latin America's tropical rainforests by two young biologists.

Jordan, Carl F. "Amazon Rain Forests." *American Scientist,* vol. 20, no. 4: 394–401.

Macdonald, David, ed. *All the World's Animals: Primates.* New York: Torstar Books, 1984.

Macdonald, David, ed. *All the World's Animals: Hoofed Mammals.* New York: Torstar Books, 1984.

McNeeley, Jeffrey A. and Kenton R. Miller, *National Parks, Conservation, and Development: The Role of Protected Areas in Sustaining Society.* Washington, D.C.: Smithsonian Institution Press, 1984.

Mitchell, Andrew W. *The Enchanted Canopy: A Journey of Discovery to the Last Unexplored Frontier, the Roof of the World's Rainforests.* New York: Macmillan, 1986.

Myers, Norman, ed. *Gaia: An Atlas of Planet Management.* Garden City, N.Y.: Anchor Press/Doubleday, 1984.
A well-illustrated explanation of our planet's environmental problems from tropical deforestation to acid rain.

Myers, Norman. *The Primary Source: Tropical Forests and Our Future.* New York: W.W. Norton, 1984.
A comprehensive, well-documented look at the future of the earth's tropical forests by one of the world's leading conservationists.

Myers, Norman. *The Sinking Ark: A New Look at the Problem of Disappearing Species.* New York: Pergamon Press, 1979.

Perry, Donald. *Life Above the Jungle Floor: A Biologist Explores a Strange and Hidden Treetop World*. New York: Simon and Schuster, 1986.
A readable and beautifully illustrated science adventure book about a biologist's research in the canopy of Costa Rica's tropical rainforest.

Smith, Nigel J. H. *Rainforest Corridors: The Transamazon Colonization Scheme*. Berkeley and Los Angeles: University of California Press, 1982.

Soulé, Michael E. and Bruce A. Wilcox, eds. *Conservation Biology: An Evolutionary-Ecological Perspective*. Sunderland, Massachusetts: Sinauer Associates, 1980.

Turnbull, Colin. *The Forest People: A Study of the Pygmies of the Congo*. New York: Simon and Schuster, 1962.
Anthropologist Turnbull's account of his research with the BaMbuti Pygmies takes the reader into the African rainforest to share the daily life of these gentle people.

White, Peter T. "Tropical Rain Forests: Nature's Dwindling Treasures." *National Geographic*, vol. 163, no. 1 (1983):2–48.

Wilson, Edward O. "Clockwork Lives of the Amazonian Leafcutter Army." *Smithsonian* (October 1984): 93–100.

World Resources Institute. *Tropical Forests: A Call for Action*. Washington, D.C.: World Resources Institute, 1985.

Index

About the Author

James D. Nations is Director of Research for the Center for Human Ecology in Austin, Texas. Born in Texas, he received a Ph.D. in ecological anthropology from Southern Methodist University after three years of field research on the Lacandon Maya, a group of rainforest Indians in Chiapas, Mexico. His studies of the human use of tropical ecosystems have taken him to the rainforests of fifteen countries. This is his first book for Franklin Watts.